STUDIES IN ENGLISH LITE

General Editor

David Daiches

Already published in the series:

Already published in the series (continued):

SHAKESPEARE: OTHELLO

by
JULIET McLAUCHLAN

Teacher of English,
Aylesbury High School

EDWARD ARNOLD

© JULIET McLAUCHLAN 1971

First published 1971 by
Edward Arnold (Publishers) Ltd.,
41 Bedford Square, London WC1B 3DQ

Edward Arnold (Australia) Pty Ltd.,
80 Waverley Road, Caulfield East,
Victoria 3145, Australia

Reprinted 1975, 1979, 1981, 1983, 1985

ISBN 0 7131 5597 3

All Rights Reserved, No part of this publication may be
reproduced, stored in a retrieval system, or transmitted,
in any form or by any means, electronic, mechanical,
photocopying, recording or otherwise, without the prior
permission of Edward Arnold (Publishers) Ltd.

To Robert Ryan (Nottingham, 1967)
and Brewster Mason (Stratford-upon-Avon, 1971)

Printed and bound in Great Britain at
The Camelot Press Ltd, Southampton

General Preface

The object of this series is to provide studies of individual novels, plays and groups of poems and essays which are known to be widely read by students. The emphasis is on clarification and evaluation; biographical and historical facts, while they may be discussed when they throw light on particular elements in a writer's work, are generally subordinated to critical discussion. What kind of work is this? What exactly goes on here? How good is this work, and why? These are the questions that each writer will try to answer.

It should be emphasized that these studies are written on the assumption that the reader has already read carefully the work discussed. The objective is not to enable students to deliver opinions about works they have not read, nor is it to provide ready-made ideas to be applied to works that have been read. In one sense all critical interpretation can be regarded as foisting opinions on readers, but to accept this is to deny the advantages of any sort of critical discussion directed at students or indeed at anybody else. The aim of these studies is to provide what Coleridge called in another context 'aids to reflection' about the works discussed. The interpretations are offered as suggestive rather than as definitive, in the hope of stimulating the reader into developing further his own insights. This is after all the function of all critical discourse among sensible people.

Because of the interest which this kind of study has aroused, it has been decided to extend it first from merely English literature to include also some selected works of American literature and now further to include selected works in English by Commonwealth writers. The criterion will remain that the book studied is important in itself and is widely read by students.

DAVID DAICHES

Contents

* This comprises chapter and general bibliographies.

1. The Starting Point

Too often textual problems are seen as the concern of the textual specialist only, and are pushed aside as something of a bore by the student or critic who cannot wait to get down to what seems more exciting in Shakespeare: 'plot', 'character', 'poetry', or 'drama'—which may too often be studied quite separately. Some Shakespearian criticism begins and ends with character analysis. Yet Shakespeare's characters are figures in a poetic and dramatic whole, not living people or historical personages. They act within 'the providence of the plot', so it is vital to see them as inseparable from the movement of this plot and from the shape of the play as a whole.

The starting point for all who study Shakespeare's plays in their modern texts, and love them in the theatre, must be the text itself. John Dover Wilson (in his Introduction to the Cambridge *Hamlet*, 1934) points out that the understanding of character and plot depends on a prior understanding of what characters are actually saying: establishing the text must come first. Then follow three stages which Dover Wilson clearly enumerates: interpretation of dialogue; elucidation of plot; finally, estimation of character. I prefer to see the three as quite inseparable within the dramatic and poetic whole of the established text.

The Text of 'Othello'

The First Quarto was published in 1622; the First Folio in 1623 as part of the first collected edition of all Shakespeare's plays except *Pericles*. These are the two basic texts and, although neither is universally accepted as 'good', neither can be regarded as 'bad'; each counts eminent critics among its advocates. The Second Quarto (1630) is generally agreed to provide us with Q1 as corrected by close collation with F. Besides including passages not found in Q1, Q2 is of great interest as an edited text which can readily be compared with F and Q1. The later Folios and Quartos, offering only editorial emendations, do not contribute to the establishment of a more authoritative text, although they do give us the benefit of considered judgements of individual editors. Since neither F nor Qı is wholly satisfactory, each new edition of *Othello* must be an eclectic one, and individual judgements must continue to be made.

To a lesser degree, similar judgements have to be made by the literary critic. Detailed discussion of textual problems is inappropriate to a primarily literary critique but, since criticism depends upon textual reading, acquaintance with the earliest texts is both interesting and necessary. Though relying greatly upon the specialised knowledge and findings of textual critics, the literary critic may at times have a contribution to make. Indeed it would be wrong to suggest too absolute a distinction between the two: textual critics are often literary critics, and vice versa; some combination of the two is always essential. Any serious attempt to see the pattern of a Shakespearian play may help when it comes to making a crucial textual choice, because one word, phrase, or line may well seem to be more consistent than another with what happens in the play as a poetic and dramatic whole. One such crux occurs in *Othello* at III, iii, 392 (*cf.* p. 46).

To the literary critic considering the problems of the text, what is most striking and, at first, depressing is that there are so many obvious possibilities of error in the seventeenth century texts which have come down to us. Ridley summarises some of these 'types of corruption or alteration' which range 'from the certain through the probable to the possible':

> blunders due to mere carelessness of compositor or transcriber (certain) or to well-meaning but unsuccessful attempts by either to make sense of illegible copy (highly probable); errors due to reliance on memory (probable, but, with our data, not provable; it is almost solely a transcriber's, not a compositor's type of error, and its first begetter is usually an actor); changes made by the author himself (no doubt quite possible . . .); would-be improvements made by others than the author (almost certain).[1]

We have no conclusive evidence as to what sort of MS. or MSS. may have been originals for F and Qı, and we must assume the existence of one or more transcripts which have come in between each of the originals and the published texts. Textual critics agree that we cannot establish any single truly authoritative text of *Othello*.

What is, therefore, most remarkable (indeed, in the light of all this,

[1] New Arden *Othello*, p. xxxii.

almost unbelievable) is that when one reads through the three versions of
Othello (F, Q1, Q2) and imagines each in performance, it is *not* the many
differences which most impress one, but the similarities. Many passages
which are long and of crucial importance to the poetic and dramatic
whole are virtually identical in all three.

One small but interesting variation (which results simply from different punctuation) comes in the first scene of Act IV, when Othello's love
is battling with his suspicion. As he is needled by Iago towards revenge,
he keeps agreeing with him, but then recalls many things which he loves
about his wife. F punctuates these with an interrogation mark. On the stage
this would have the effect of heightening the element of appeal to Iago
(*cf.* p. 49). Interrogation makes Othello beg more strongly for Iago's
assent (she *is* these things, is she not?), and Iago's refusal of any positive
response becomes more of a refusal and more cruel.

Q1 lacks one hundred and sixty lines found in F, and the lack
of some of these is serious. Most serious, in III, iii, 460–7, the
'Pontic sea' simile is lost. Significantly, there is a related loss at
V, ii, 267–72, which includes 'the sea-mark of my utmost sail',
a phrase so important to sustain the 'labouring bark' image—as
indeed both of these omissions are. Desdemona's speech at IV, ii, loses
lines 153–66 ('Here I kneel . . .'). We miss here the emphasis on the oath
she is taking; kneeling, she swears to her innocence by all she holds
sacred. Something of Iago's cruelty is also lost if we do not see him stand
there, watching her, and listening to her, and then at the end showing
himself to be as unrelenting as ever.

The Dating of 'Othello'

Precise dating is not possible, but the consensus of opinion places it
certainly not earlier than 1602; 1603 seems more likely, and its first performance was almost certainly in 1604. In any case, it comes firmly
between *Hamlet* and *King Lear*. For both of these plays we have early
Quartos. There is none for *Othello*, but this does not mean that the long
gap between its writing and its publication is unique. For *Antony and
Cleopatra*, *The Winter's Tale*, and many other plays we have only the
Folio text. What is interesting about *Othello* is that after a gap of eighteen
to twenty years, we have the publication of a late Quarto and of the
Folio within a year of each other and since, in all probability, they came
from different originals, there would seem to have been every chance for

wide and indeed crucial variations. Only the power of Shakespeare's dramatic conception, together with the extraordinary consistency and force of the language which gave it form, could have made possible the survival of so fine an *Othello* (despite minor variants and some controversial points) as the one we can know through these texts.

My references to *Othello* will be to the New Arden edition (Methuen, 1958).

2. *Approaching the Play: the Language*

Since most major critics, past and present, have written about *Othello*, it would be unnecessary, even presumptuous, to write yet more if there were nothing to add to the understanding and appreciation of one of Shakespeare's greatest tragedies. For two reasons there is much to add: certain aspects of the play have received far too little critical attention, or none at all; many critics, including eminent and influential ones, have supported dubious points of view by lifting a few lines here and there out of their context. Some disastrous misconceptions have resulted, because each of Shakespeare's plays is a unified whole and must be seen as such, whether it is watched on the stage or studied as a text. *Othello* suffers particularly if not so considered, because the tragedy is patterned with marvellous consistency.

Othello is often considered to be the simplest of Shakespeare's great tragedies, yet, if so, it is strange that so much critical controversy should centre on it, and especially on Othello himself. Through the haze of conflicting critical comment it is very difficult to see the nature of the man and of the tragedy. In what does the tragedy of Othello consist? How far is the tragedy seen to come about by the plotting of Iago and how far by faults in Othello's nature? What are these faults? Do racial, social, or any other factors contribute? There are many aspects to the tragedy, but I shall argue that the essence of it lies in the interaction of qualities in Othello and in Iago. The tragedy is that a man of Othello's positive qualities should possess weaknesses upon which Iago is uniquely qualified to play; that Iago, through knowledge of his victim's nature, does this in such ways as to rouse latent destructive passions in Othello. There is little in this, so far, to rouse controversy, but I shall further argue that *what the text shows* (and what an audience should see on the stage) is an Othello 'wrought' to a pitch of anguish and confusion so terrible that it temporarily overmasters all that is fine in him and brings him to destroy what he most loves, yet that *the text also shows* an Othello 'not easily jealous' though certainly 'perplex'd in the extreme'. It will be necessary to question some longstanding critical misconceptions which have carried, and continue to carry, great weight. This questioning does not spring from wrong-headedness or impertinence, but from certainty that the textual pattern of Othello clearly shows certain views to be simply untenable. These will be referred to as they arise in the course of this study.

The aspects of the play which have not had sufficiently detailed critical attention are: the significance of the storm and of storm imagery; the significance of heaven-and-hell imagery; the 'brawl' scene (II, iii) as a key to Othello's nature, to the basis of his trust in Iago, and therefore to the tragedy as a whole; the significance of the handkerchief; the crucial alterations which Shakespeare made to Giraldi Cinthio's tale. The most serious critical misconceptions have arisen from misunderstanding of Othello's nature, especially of the quality of his love for Desdemona.

A play, even a Shakespearian play, is primarily a dramatic whole, not a sacred text. Reading and studying Shakespeare, one should never lose sight of this, but from time to time test the consistency of ideas about the play by imagining them in actual dramatic presentation as part of a dramatic whole. This is not to minimise the importance of the words themselves. They give to the story (a poor melodramatic thing, by comparison) its form—Shakespeare's form. In *Othello* the choice of words and variations of style are essential to the whole artistic creation, providing the key to character and theme, and therefore to the whole pattern of the tragedy. An ideal production of *Othello* (or of any of Shakespeare's plays) would be one in which the beauties of the text were so understood and *realised* by the actors as to make a consistently satisfying whole. I shall not attempt to outline such a production *in toto*, but from time to time cite instances in which a certain emphasis in the dramatic presentation seems to be called for by the language.

What I shall always be arguing is that in *Othello* the force of the language is such that it must (if understood) impose upon actors certain types of behaviour. This is not to suggest that there will be just one way of acting any part in a particular scene, but that the language must define a *permissible range*, as it were. It is a serious mistake to separate Shakespeare's poetry from his drama. As M. C. Bradbrook points out:

> The Elizabethans hardly used stage directions at all, because the action, though important, was not intended to define the feelings but to reflect *those defined in the verse*.[1] (my italics)

It was because of a general interest in language that Elizabethan playwrights could so well build their drama on words. Elizabethan audiences were quite different from present-day ones in their approach to drama, being accustomed to look for poetic patterns and to follow the action in this way. Stylistic devices were used to coat pills of moral truth, and rules of style were based on classical theories of rhetoric, which were widely studied in schools. The age was one of language games; of poetry written to fit into given shapes; of word coinages; of widespread interest in dialects and foreign languages.

Educated people had much better vocabularies than the rest, but all classes were interested in language. We see evidence of this when Shakespeare shows amusing misuse of words by such characters as Dogberry (in *Much Ado*), the nurse (in *Romeo and Juliet*) and the gravedigger (in *Hamlet*)—with, also, the gravedigger's delight in word-play.

Bearing in mind the sort of audiences for whom Shakespeare wrote plays, we can see then that we are not going too far if we look very closely into his use of language: the language is the drama.

3. The Tragic Pattern

The Storm

Precisely what is to *happen* in the tragedy is prefigured in the imagery associated with the storm. Theodore Spencer aptly refers to it as 'a foretaste—a chaos in the macrocosm—of what is to happen in Othello's

[1] *Themes and Conventions of Elizabethan Tragedy*, p. 43.

soul'.[1] In Cinthio's story all the main characters cross together and there is no storm.[2] This Shakespearian innovation is vital: the poetry in which he evokes the menacing, treacherous, destructive power of *this* storm is impressive and cannot be regarded as merely decorative.

For the crossing, Othello entrusts Desdemona to Iago's care. In this 'foul and violent tempest' the

> Tempests themselves, high seas, and howling winds,
> The gutter'd rocks, and congregated sands,
> Traitors ensteep'd to clog the guiltless keel,
> As having sense of beauty, do omit
> Their common[3] nature, as letting go safely by
> The divine Desdemona. (II, i, 68–73)

Whether attributed to Cassio (F) or the Second Gentleman (Q1), this speech is more than formal hyperbolic compliment. Its heavy ironies are reinforced by other references to the storm and are echoed verbally later in the play (*cf.* IV, i, 45–7 and V, ii, 123).

Through his trust in Iago, Othello unwittingly continues to entrust Desdemona to him, and thus, with fatal consequences, to the fury of the later storm. This, although it takes on its own terrible force, yet is entirely controlled by Iago, for he and he alone has the power at any stage to restore calm. It sweeps the nature of Othello and does not let Desdemona go unharmed. Iago, unlike the lurking treacherous dangers of the sea, does not 'omit' his 'common nature' to spare her. Before Cassio's arrival, the First Gentleman speaks of the 'high-wrought' flood, echoed at the end of the play in Othello's apt reference to himself as 'wrought'.

There is particular irony in many of Cassio's words; they prefigure the tragic and final separation which the later storm will bring between himself and Othello. Cassio prays that

> . . . the heavens give him defence against their elements
> For I have lost him on a dangerous sea (II, i, 44–6)

and later declares:

---

[1] *Shakespeare and the Nature of Man*, p. 125.
[2] '. . . e con somma tranquillità del Mare, si andò in Cipri', Furness *Variorum*, p. 378.
[3] 'Mortal' (Qq) brings in the sense of fatal or deadly, which is apt, but I prefer F's 'common': taking this to mean ordinary or usual, the omission seems very exceptional, almost miraculous.

>   ... the great contention of the sea, and skies
>   Parted our fellowship. (II, i, 92–3)

Their 'fellowship' is later savagely parted through the work of Iago, first
in the relatively minor incident of the cashiering, later by the 'elements'
in Othello himself. These storm to the surface and against the very
heavens—heavens which provide 'defence' for neither Othello himself
nor for Desdemona.

It is in the calm aftermath of the storm that irory reaches the peak of
poignancy, in Othello's beautiful words to his 'fair warrior'. Speaking of
his 'wonder' great as his 'content', he goes on:

>   ... O my soul's joy,
>   If after every tempest come such calmness,
>   May the winds blow, till they have waken'd death,
>   And let the labouring bark climb hills of seas
>   Olympus-high, and duck again as low
>   As hell's from heaven.[4] (II, i, 183–9)

The metaphor of Othello's 'labouring bark' is sustained, and becomes
most moving at the play's end. In the actual storm Montano questions
the ability of any 'ribs of oak' to 'hold the mortise', 'when mountains
melt on them'. Cassio, although worried too, takes comfort because
'[Othello's] bark is stoutly timbered, and [significantly] his pilot /Of very
expert and approved allowance'. Nothing can be seen ''twixt the heaven
and the main'; the elements seem to be threatening to 'cast water on the
burning bear' and 'Quench the guards of the ever fixed [Qq, 'fired']
pole'. The guards, two stars in the Little Bear, were very important
guides to navigation. The storm brings such a confusion of the sea and
sky that these are threatened or lost to sight. A similar dangerous confusion in the psychological world is prefigured in Othello's words later:

>   ... Now by heaven
>   My blood begins my safer guides to rule,
>   And passion having my best judgement collied[5]
>   Assays to lead the way. (II, iii, 195–8)

----

[4] There is an interesting similarity between Othello's speech and a
passage from Sidney's *Arcadia*, Bk. I: 'The sea making mountains of itself,
over which the tossed and towering ships shoulde climbe, to be straight
carried downe againe to a pit of hellish darkness', Furness *Variorum*, p. 113.

[5] Cf. *Midsummer Night's Dream*, I, i. 'Collied' comes from a verb meaning to blacken as with coal: hence, darkened.

This is what happens later when passion and 'blood' do overrule Othello's 'judgement', or pilot. Once this flood is 'high-wrought', Othello cries 'Blood! Blood! Blood!' and expresses the compulsive force of the 'bloody thoughts' which are sweeping him along relentlessly, by comparing them with the Pontic sea (cf. p. 53):

> Whose icy current and compulsive course
> Ne'er feels retiring ebb, but keeps due on

and 'with violent pace':

> Shall ne'er look back, ne'er ebb to humble love
> Till that a capable and wide revenge
> Swallow them up . . . (III, iii, 461–2; 465–7)

Much later, the murder done, savage rage having ebbed 'to humble love', the labouring bark is at the end of its voyage:

> Here is my journey's end, here is my butt
> And very sea-mark of my utmost sail
> . . . Where should Othello go? (V, ii, 268–9, 272)

Calm after the psychological tempest has not come till winds of passion have indeed 'waken'd death' and brought the labouring bark to a state 'as low as hell's from heaven'. From his heavenly joy in Desdemona's love, Othello has been brought down to the hell of monstrous vengeance, and finally to belief in his own inevitable and just damnation.

Heaven and Hell

Contrasts between heaven and hell run right through the pattern of *Othello*.

The 'divine Desdemona' is from first to last a figure of heavenly purity and goodness. Cassio's words of welcome to her, 'Hail to thee, lady' are specifically religious in connotation and he goes on to pray that:

> . . . the grace of heaven
> Before, behind thee, and on every hand
> Enwheel thee round! (II, i, 85–7)

Desdemona herself regularly and with great earnestness appeals to heaven. Under Othello's accusations, she repeatedly protests her innocence by the most solemn oaths: 'By heaven, you do wrong me'; 'No, as I am a Christian'; 'No, as I shall be saved' (IV, ii, 83, 84, 88). She is, as Emilia cries at the end, 'heavenly true'. (Indeed, only two of Shakespeare's other heroines, through the rather different imagery associated with them, are invested with such spiritual worth: Hermione and Cordelia.)

Iago is from start to finish a 'hellish villain'. He swears by the 'divinity of Hell' (II, iii, 341) and has earlier suggested to Roderigo that his 'wits' are working with 'all the tribe of hell' (I, iii, 358). He makes his position even clearer:

> When devils will the blackest sins put on
> They do suggest at first with heavenly shows
> As I do now . . . (II, iii, 342–4)

It is within Othello's soul that we watch 'the great contention of seas and skies', of hellish and heavenly forces. The tragedy which the audience should feel is that at the beginning Othello is shown with no inclination towards the hellish, the devilish, the 'monstrous' which gradually gain possession of him 'body and soul' as he falls under Iago's influence. It is natural to him to refer to heaven in the seriousness and simplicity of his faith: he says he speaks 'as truly as to heaven I do confess the vices of my blood'. When he swears by heaven (I, iii, 261–7), his obvious sincerity adds great weight.

Interestingly, some words of Iago's emphasise the depth of Othello's faith. He says Othello's love for Desdemona is so great that she can do what she likes with him, even:

> . . . win the Moor, were't to renounce his baptism,
> All seals and symbols of redeemed sin. (II, iii, 334–5)

This can be taken as true because Iago mentions it only to emphasise to Cassio the strength of Desdemona's influence.

In Othello's mind, Desdemona's appearance and nature are heavenly; after becoming suspicious, he cries out in anguish at the sight of her:

> If she be false, O, then heaven mocks itself,
> I'll not believe it. (III, iii, 282–3)

Once Iago has convinced him of her guilt, he calls: 'Arise, black vengeance, from the hollow hell'. Whether we accept this reading (F) or the variant (Qq) 'from thy hollow cell', there is the same idea of hellish depths and the same contrast with the preceding line when he has blown 'to heaven' all his 'fond love' (III, iii, 452–4). Iago has won him to hellish feelings and to the contemplation of fiendish vengeance. It is a terrible moment when he then solemnly swears 'by yond marble heaven'.

For Desdemona has now become 'fair devil' (III, iii, 485), and Othello calls her 'devil' (IV, i, 235, 239) more than once before striking her publicly. By the brothel scene he has sunk even lower and can assure her that 'Heaven truly knows that thou art false as hell' (IV, ii, 40). Heaven and hell are now so confused in his mind (as were the sea and sky in the storm) that he associates the heavenly Desdemona more and more closely with evil and hell. At the end of this scene he calls Emilia 'You . . . that keep the gate of hell' (IV, ii, 92–4). Having come to believe Desdemona to be impure, he feels he *is* in hell.

What gives most force to the heaven-hell imagery is that Othello is shown to believe in actual damnation; it is vivid and real to him. Before killing Desdemona, he tries to persuade her to confess her guilt and to ask for heaven's grace and pardon. He insists, for:

> I would not kill thy unprepared spirit:
> No, heaven forfend! I would not kill thy soul. (V, ii, 31–2)

This is a point at which an actor should underline Othello's solemn horror; similarly, the audience should be made to feel conviction behind his words, when he is later justifying his murder:

> O, I were damned beneath all depths in hell,
> But that I did proceed upon just grounds
> To the extremity: . . . (V, ii, 138–40)

As soon as he then finds out his tragic mistake, he has no alternative but to see himself as damned to the 'burning hell' in which he believes. Looking upon the beauty of his dead wife, conscious now of her innocence, he thinks first of the Day of Judgement:

> When we shall meet at count
> This look of thine will hurl my soul from heaven
> And fiends will snatch at it

and he then calls upon the powers of hell to come at once:

> Whip me, ye devils,
> From the possession of this heavenly sight!
> Blow me about in winds! roast me in sulphur!
> Wash me in steep-down gulfs of liquid fire! (V, ii, 274–5; 278–81)

This is not empty rhetoric or self-dramatisation. Taking his own life, Othello believes that he is thus consigning both soul and body to the literal torments of hell ('perdition') just as he has imagined them.

The Pattern

Themes and motifs in *Othello* are worked out through finely-contrasted scenes (to which a full-length study might well be devoted). As a dramatic whole, the play develops in major movements. The waves of Iago's attack break first against, then over, Othello, to work finally through him to overwhelm Desdemona.

In the play's first scene the first wave is set in motion with Iago's dark plotting in dark streets. After his success with Roderigo and Brabantio, the second prong of this attack is directed towards Othello. Scene 2 is still dark, but its atmosphere is totally transformed by the calm beauty of Othello's presence. This presence is even more impressive as the next scene shifts to the bright public setting of the council chamber. The first wave has left Othello unmoved: 'more fair than black', he seems indeed unassailable, whether privately or publicly.

Act II opens under an ominously lowering sky, to the sounds of the storm: elemental fury modulates to tension as we wait for both Desdemona and Othello to arrive safely; tension modulates to the radiance of the reunion scene, which is shadowed at once by the threat of Iago's developing plan. The second wave gathers force in the violence of the brawl, again in dark streets: Othello's anger is temporarily roused, but soon ebbs, and both the private and the public Othello seem still untouched. We see Iago, however, preparing the next wave of the attack, on the basis of what has happened.

Act III opens with an early morning scene in which the need for Iago's further action becomes evident, as Cassio learns from both Emilia and Desdemona of Othello's virtual promise to restore him to his position as soon as it may be politic. Before the third great wave of the 'temptation', we see Othello quietly carrying out routine military duties and talking lovingly with Desdemona. This is the last time we are to see the private and the public man unmoved.

The third wave gathers momentum gradually, in perceptible movements, working more and more through Othello himself. Doubts and confusion come first; as these deepen, the public Othello begins to be affected (his 'occupation' loses all value once his love seems corrupt). Vengeful anger is roused, and the storm for the first time extends to Desdemona; after the complete internal 'chaos' which culminates in his fit, comes the terrible spectacle of Othello, now almost Iago's creature, spying and muttering in the street. Othello's determination to have revenge is strengthened here, but this ebbs to humble love as he appeals to Iago (cf. p. 49); we see here his last real resistance to the attack. Public disintegration goes a stage further and the storm (now operating directly through Othello) extends to Desdemona with more violence as Othello strikes her publicly. In the brothel scene, tears, confusion and anger rage together, with no ebbing to love but only lamenting for love's corruption. Desdemona has felt the full force of this: stunned ('half asleep'), she appeals to Iago (cf. p. 24). The quiet pathos of the next scene with Emilia is almost unendurable, since we know that Iago will not act to call back forces he has set in motion: this is the final lull before destructive fury must break over Desdemona. A fitting prelude to the murder is Iago's violent physical attack on Cassio and Roderigo, again in dark streets; then Othello's private chaos culminates in passionate grief, jealousy, and the extinction of Desdemona's life. Rage first ebbs slightly as it mingles with grief; agonised defence of the deed gives way in turn to despair, self-destruction, and the final ebb to love as Othello dies upon a kiss.

A Note on Race

Othello's colour is far from being the decisive factor, but it is a vital element in Shakespeare's whole conception of the tragic pattern. Winthrop Jordan's comments (in a book mainly concerned with the early history of the American negro) are illuminating:

> The measure of influence exerted upon English commentators by these Hebraic traditions [in which heightened sexual powers and brutality were commonly associated with dark people] is problematical, but it is certain that the presumption of heightened sexuality in black men was far from being an incidental or casual association in the minds of Englishmen. How very deeply this association operated is obvious in *Othello*, a drama which loses most of its power and several of its central points if it is read with the assumption that because the black man was the hero English audiences were friendly or perhaps indifferent to his blackness. . . . Shakespeare did not condemn such unions: rather, he played upon an inner theme of black and white sexuality, showing how the poisonous mind of a white man perverted and destroyed the noblest of lovers by means of bringing to the surface (from the darkness whence Iago spoke) the lurking shadows of animal sex to assault the whiteness of chastity. Never did 'dirty' words more dramatically 'blacken' a 'fair' name . . . Shakespeare's genius lay

precisely in juxtaposing these two pairs: inner blackness and inner whiteness.[6]

Rather similarly, R. B. Heilman in a very subtle and distinguished essay (see Bibliography) speaks of the 'paradox' in *Othello*: that of 'black as fair' (Othello at the beginning) and 'fair as foul' (Desdemona's white purity made by Iago to seem foul). One might add that Iago himself is 'fair as black', his fair exterior covering his black and poisonous nature.

Eldred Jones, too, sees an antithesis in the presentation of Iago: he appears to be simply a plain soldier, but 'I am not what I am'. As for Othello:

> He is taken (by some of the characters) as the manifestation of a type—barbarous Moor, bond-slave, pagan—and he turns out to be noble Christian, if somewhat naïve. We thus have a double antithesis: Iago is both soldier and villain, Othello is both Moor and noble hero.[7]

Jones's book is as a whole most interesting for its comments on Elizabethan attitudes to dark people and on the presentation in Elizabethan drama of coloured characters other than Othello.

A chapter on *Othello* in Philip Mason's book is of interest, too, for the emphasis it places on racial prejudice within the play on the part of Iago, Brabantio, and Roderigo.

It is fascinating the way Shakespeare presented his audiences with two figures which were virtual stereotypes and proceeded to reverse completely the normal expectations of the way they should act.

Assuming some degree of racial prejudice both inside the play and in Shakespeare's audiences (and even today), we can see the dramatic necessity for Othello to make a certain kind of impression in the early scenes. The language is such as to convey perfectly his nobility of soul and inner whiteness: the actor of Othello must so project this that the audience responds deeply to the Duke's final words to Brabantio:

> If virtue no delighted beauty lack,
> Your son-in-law is far more fair than black. (I, iii, 289–90)

---

[6] *White Over Black*, pp. 37, 38.   [7] *Othello's People*, p. 108.

4. Why?

Why does the tragedy come about? There is no answer in the text to this question—to why, that is, Iago acts as he does. In *Othello* (as in *King Lear* on a vaster scale) the mystery of evil looms behind the tragic events:

Then let them anatomize Regan to see what breeds about her heart. Is there any cause in nature that makes these hard hearts?

(King Lear, III, vi)

We feel something of the same mystery in *Othello*. Is there any cause in nature for evil such as Iago's? He is given much less direct and obvious causes for his behaviour than Cinthio's ensign. Iago's tortuous explanations for his plotting seem too shifting and trivial to account for the wilful torture in which he indulges with such pleasure. Caroline Spurgeon calls both *King Lear* and *Othello* 'studies of torture', with the latter the 'wanton torture of one human being by another'.[1] Significantly, Lear and Othello are the two Shakespearian heroes who are metaphorically 'on the rack'.

What is perhaps most horrifying about Iago's plotting is that it so plainly *is* a pleasure to him—a terrible and very enjoyable game he plays. A key scene culminates in his remark to Roderigo (before whom, more than anyone else, he allows himself to speak freely):

. . . By the mass, 'tis morning;
Pleasure and action make the hours seem short. (II, iii, 368–9)

The island has been in an uproar, Montano has been wounded, Cassio shamed and cashiered, Othello disturbed and angered—all by Iago's efforts—and this to him has been a night of pleasure. There are three scenes in which this quality in Iago can be shown effectively on the stage. The first comes in the play's opening scene, when Iago prompts Roderigo

[1] *Shakespeare's Imagery*, p. 336.

to rouse Brabantio, then enters into it all with great energy and enthusiasm, until he finally withdraws to rejoin Othello so as not to incriminate himself. In the brawl scene (indeed in the whole of II, iii) we see the same thing on a larger scale. Finally, in the opening scene of the last act, Iago is again seen in frenzied activity, but now, grown desperate, he ruthlessly maims Cassio and kills Roderigo. His manipulation is more deadly to others, his ugliness more nakedly evident, but Iago should still show a kind of perverse enjoyment in his actions even though 'This is the night/That either makes me or fordoes me quite'. As early as I, iii, 401–2, his plot 'engendr'd', he has told us 'Hell and night/must bring this monstrous birth to the world's light', and it is dramatically fitting that these scenes be played on the modern stage in near-darkness, to suggest the black and hellish nature of the confused movement, shouting, injury and death, which result from Iago's machinations. (Since this was not possible on the Elizabethan stage, the language which *suggests* all these things was even more important.)

There is a further aspect of the mystery of evil in *Othello*. Nothing prevents the 'hellish villain' from acting as he does, or from succeeding, even though Cassio, Desdemona, Othello (before his nature is swept by hellish passions), even Emilia, earnestly call upon heaven for blessing and protection. The heavens do not intervene. Unlike Leontes, whose sins are less excusable (*cf.* Appendix C), Othello is not granted a period of repentance or any regained happiness. There is no explanation in the text.

We cannot explain why Iago acts as he does, or why he is permitted to succeed, but there is much to consider in this complex character.

Devil and Vice

With regard to Iago and two other characters in *Othello*, the *Dramatis Personae* of the Folios and Quartos was more helpfully explicit than our modern texts and playbills: Cassio, now simply 'Othello's lieutenant', was 'an Honourable Lieutenant'; Roderigo, now 'a Venetian gentleman', was 'a gull'd gentleman'; Iago, now 'Othello's ancient', was plainly and simply 'a Villaine'.

Plain enough—but what sort of 'villain'? If tempted to puzzle unduly over his villainy, we should realise that Elizabethan audiences would have been less puzzled: they expected a villain to *be* a villain, and it was not essential for him to be clearly motivated. Similarly, they would have been less surprised that Iago should be believed: the credibility of the calumniator was a convention as widely accepted as the impenetrability of disguise. Closely as the imagery associates Iago's nature and actions with the devilish and hellish, *Othello* is not an allegory, with Iago as simply devil or bad angel, and Desdemona as Othello's good angel. In a useful article, Leah Scragg notes that Iago

> has been variously regarded as a Devil on a metaphysical level, as a Devil incarnate, as a man possessed, and as a man in the process of becoming a Devil by denial of the basic facts of his humanity.[2]

Any of these views would imply that Shakespeare wrote *Othello* within a consciously theological framework—a framework, moreover, requiring belief in the existence of real devils. Mrs. Scragg herself sensibly sees Iago's devilish nature and behaviour more in terms of his stage ancestry, the Devil of the Mystery Plays. Characteristic of these, and particularly reminiscent of Iago with his desire to 'set down the pegs that make this music' (II, i, 200), is the Serpent in the Norwich Mystery Cycle, who says he 'can yt not abyde, in their joye they shulde be'. Mrs. Scragg sees Iago as 'malevolent in the extreme', and her argument is most interesting.

> The proposal that Iago is a Devil in some sense of the word implies that it is his nature to envy those whose character or situation is in any way superior to his own, to suffer from a sense of injured merit and to seek to destroy anything which by its very superiority threatens his self-love. Hence, locally, he feels he has been slighted by Othello in the promotion of Cassio, he asserts that Othello and Cassio have cuckolded him from his conviction that they cannot be as virtuous as they appear, and from his diseased belief that he is being constantly slighted. . . . At the close of the play when he has corrupted Othello's mind, destroyed both him and Desdemona, when for them Paradise has been lost, Iago is dragged away to the tortures that are his element. He does not die at the end of the play. . . . He is to linger in pain like the powers of which he is an instrument. . . .[3]

Iago's stage descent, then, she sees as being much more from the Mystery Devil than from the Morality Vice. He plainly inherits and embodies some traits of the Vice: delight in his own skill; regarding his actvities as 'sport'; desire to bring down his victim to ruin; careful

[2] 'Iago, Vice or Devil?', *Shakespeare Survey*, 21, p. 65.
[3] *SS*, 21, p. 64.

pretence of being the victims' friend, but the Devils often shared these characteristics, and the great gain from emphasising Iago-as-Devil is that he thereby becomes 'motivated antagonist', not just 'unmotivated seducer'. Even more important, although as a human being his attitude seems simply amoral, he becomes an immoral rather than an amoral being. To show that in intention he is no mere 'gay, light-hearted intriguer' (the Vice), one speech is conclusive:

> And by how much she strives to do him good,
> She shall undo her credit with the Moor;
> So will I turn her virtue into pitch,
> And out of her own goodness make the net
> That shall enmesh 'em all. (II, III, 349-53)

This point needs emphasis, because critics have maintained that Iago does not really mean much harm, but somehow things gradually get out of hand and develop into tragedy. It is probably true that he does not start out with the full horror of the final tragedy as his aim, but if we doubt his unrelenting malevolence, we have only to think of his heartless rejection of Othello's broken-hearted appeal 'O, Iago, the pity of it, Iago' (IV, i, 192) and of the stricken Desdemona's appeal only a little later:

> O, good Iago
> What shall I do to win my lord again?
> Good friend, go to him . . . (IV, ii, 150-2)

These two scenes are unmatched in all tragedy: they are almost too painful to watch on the stage, for we feel that we are passing through the last moments when the tragedy might still be averted; we watch in horror this torturer, his victims in agony before his eyes, trusting him wholly—and he is quite unrelenting. Some critics have expressed the view that Iago should show some emotional response, momentary embarrassment, hesitation, in this last scene with Desdemona, but this would be quite out of character. Iago's actions and words are those of 'a moral being impelled by a burning desire to feed fat a consuming hatred for the good and beautiful with revenge'.[4]

4 *SS*, 21, p. 63.

Machiavel

It is clear that the Vice and Devil are important elements in Iago's stage ancestry, and Elizabethans would have been much more aware of this than modern audiences. It follows that it is not enough to explain Iago's villainy by seeing him as simply one of a long line of Machiavels. In the rest of my discussion, the word will mean only the sort of speech, 'practice', and behaviour of *stage* 'Machiavels'. The connection between this and what Machiavelli wrote is pretty tenuous (see Bibliography). Machiavellian Iago *is* in his manipulation of people, but in *The Prince* (1513) Machiavelli wrote of the behaviour proper to people in very high positions, who meant at all costs to remain in authority. We see in Elizabethan and Jacobean tragedy very much the English conception of Machiavellism; in this sense, the villain-hero, Richard III (a pre-*Othello* play) and Edmund (in *King Lear*, written a year or so after *Othello*) are more truly Machiavels than Iago. They are both concerned with ambition and kingly power—with gaining control of the state and keeping it by unscrupulous and ruthless means.

Wyndham Lewis comments on the tremendous influence of Machiavelli in England, and he quotes Dr. Grosart as saying that 'he came to be regarded as an incarnation of the Evil One himself.'⁵ Elizabethan audiences would be aware of this when watching Iago. This makes it all the more interesting that Shakespeare should have brought together in Iago the vicious, the diabolical, and the Machiavellian.

For some idea of what the stage Machiavel was like before Shakespeare, we can look to Villuppo and Lorenzo in Kyd's *The Spanish Tragedy*. Because precise dating of this play has not been possible, it can be placed with certainty only between 1582 and 1592, the most likely date being in the mid or late eighties. Marlowe's *The Jew of Malta* has not been precisely dated either, though it was first performed in 1591, so we cannot be sure which shows the first of the Machiavels. Marlowe sums up his villain:

> . . . you shall find him still,
> In all his projects, a sound Machiavill;
> And that's his character . . .
>
> (The Prologue Spoken at Court, *The Jew of Malta*)

⁵ *The Lion and the Fox*, p. 66.

In Kyd's play, after Villuppo has successfully thrown blame for Baltha-
zar's supposed death on Alexandro, Villuppo gloats:

> Thus have I with an envious forged tale
> Deceived the king, betrayed mine enemy,
> And hope for guerdon of my villainy. (I, iii)

Found out quite soon, he makes clear that he has been motivated simply
by the desire for 'reward and hope to be preferred' (III, i).

Interestingly, the spirit of Revenge, personified and speaking from
time to time as Chorus, oversees and controls the action of the play and
speaks in Machiavellian terms:

> I'll turn their friendship into fell despite,
> Their love to mortal hate, their day to night,
> Their hope into despair, their peace to war,
> Their joys to pain, their bliss to misery (I, v)

Succeeding for a time, Lorenzo gloats in Machiavellian fashion:

> I lay the plot, he prosecutes the point;
> I set the trap, he breaks the worthless twigs,
> And sees not that wherewith the bird was limed . . . (III, iv)

Similarities to Iago are obvious, but Iago as Machiavel is in
important ways different from any of the other many villains of the
Elizabethan and Jacobean stage. It is usual for the Machiavel to victim-
ise, torment, torture, or kill good people (or less good people) or, by
manipulation, to prompt weak or wicked people to do vile deeds against
the innocent. This is true in the pre-Shakespeare plays cited, and in
The Duchess of Malfi (1613–14). In the latter, the duchess is tormented
and ultimately killed on her brothers' orders by their instrument,
Bosola. Although Webster suggests something of the *Othello* heaven-
hell antithesis insofar as 'the devil speaks' in the brothers, and the duchess's
'nights . . . her very sleep / Are more in heaven than are other ladies'
shrifts' (I, i), the play shows a plain attack of evil on innocence. Iago
is uniquely evil and horrible: he does not himself torment and kill the
good, or do evil through evil instruments, but works by manipulation
of what is mainly good.

Even the gull Roderigo, a weak and foolish tool, has good points. He
wishes at first to marry Desdemona, and believes her to be 'of most blest
condition' until Iago convinces him that she may be false. Emilia is used
by Iago in furthering his schemes, but it is only her wish to please (and

perhaps placate) a difficult husband which prompts her to give him Desdemona's handkerchief. Her failure to realise the seriousness of Desdemona's distress and of Othello's anger are more blameworthy, but her horror and revulsion when she discovers her husband's wickedness, her fierce and selfless determination to tell the truth and clear her mistress's name are what count. They give the play some very dramatic moments and place Emilia firmly on the side of the 'good'.

In Cassio we see a good deal of the 'daily beauty' which Iago resents—chiefly in Cassio's attitude towards Othello and Desdemona. Since he is otherwise something of a light-weight, it is the more striking that his respect for his general amounts to devotion; his respect for Desdemona to reverence. The audience must feel that he is genuine. This is supremely important when Iago is needling Cassio with suggestively salacious comments on Desdemona's charms, and Cassio replies with only the greatest respect for her qualities. From all he says, the audience must draw a conviction that he is himself indeed 'honourable' and that both Desdemona and Othello are supremely worthy of his admiration. His attitude towards them is sharply differentiated from his much more familiar manner with Emilia and Iago, and even more sharply from the basically contemptuous way in which he treats his whore. Any actor playing Cassio must make these nuances evident.

Especially horrible to watch is Iago's use of Desdemona's goodness. It is, ironically, from his words that the audience learns of some of the loveliest of her qualities when he tells Cassio:

. . . She is of so free, so kind, so apt, so blessed, a disposition, that she holds it a vice in her goodness not to do more than she is requested. (II, iii, 310–13)

In soliloquy, too, he assures us that she is 'framed as fruitful as the free elements' (II, iii, 332–3)—lovely words and, like the others, they suggest that Desdemona's 'virtue', which he means to turn to 'pitch', consists of overflowing generosity, kindness, blessedness. (To Iago, 'fruitful' and 'free' may have carried grosser sexual connotations, as they often do, but the audience will be unlikely to accept them in this way.)

These are the people, not paid hirelings or willing malefactors, who unwittingly serve Iago's purpose. But the final unparalleled horror is his manipulation of Othello himself, whereby a great and noble soul is 'wrought' to vengeful murder of the 'heavenly true', and to self-destruction.

The Bluff Soldier

Machiavellism adds an important dimension to Iago as Vice and Devil, but the three together still do not account for the total realised stage personality which has for so long baffled critics. In Shakespeare's hands, something extremely complex, ambiguous, and subtle grew out of the Elizabethan ideas of villainy, surpassing their crudities and those of the Jacobean villains. What is added is the aspect of Iago as blunt soldier, bluff and 'honest'. This (a stage stereotype) is the exterior through which we sometimes see the Vice peep, behind which the Devil and Machiavel so successfully hide themselves that they can do their work quite unsuspected. Iago's diabolical manipulation succeeds precisely because this provides the perfect mask. No type could appear further removed from the Machiavel than an ordinary honest soldier with nothing of the smooth courtier to arouse distrust—whose chief fault indeed seems to be too much plain-speaking.

To understand better how Iago appears to the characters within the play (for this is what matters: outside the play we see him differently, and Elizabethan audiences would have appreciated fully the ironies of his mask), we must look at another Shakespearian soldier, Enobarbus. *Antony and Cleopatra* was written several years after *Othello*, and I do not mean to suggest that Shakespeare intended any direct contrast, but the type seems to have interested him, for between Iago and Enobarbus comes Kent, another variant of the plain-spoken and, in his case, loyal-to-the-death soldier-servant. Enobarbus plainly *is* everything which Iago merely *seems* (convincingly) to be. That is why the contrast is illuminating. Each of the two is, in a sense, the 'all-licensed fool' who sees true and whose plain-speaking is tolerated. The difference is that Enobarbus always speaks the truth, and his intentions are good. Both are cynical in manner, but Enobarbus's cynicism is a clear-sighted, amused, tolerant view of human weaknesses, Iago's a bitter and ugly assessment of human nature as base. Both have a reputation for being outspoken, but Enobarbus is more so than Iago. Enobarbus says exactly what he thinks, even to the great. Commenting cynically in the presence of both Antony and Octavius that they can 'borrow one another's love for the instant' and 'wrangle . . . when you have nothing else to do', he earns a rebuke from Antony: 'thou art a soldier: speak no more'. Enobarbus retorts: 'That truth should be silent, I had almost forgot.' This brings another rebuke from Antony, whereupon Enobarbus subsides, 'Your considerate stone' (II, ii). Iago's outspokenness is mainly pretence. He cultivates the notion that he is plain-spoken, but he shows neither the desire nor the courage to argue openly with his superiors or to stand up to them.

Enobarbus is a Roman soldier, Iago a Venetian, and they are of quite different periods, but the important point is that in both plays the bluff soldier is not only (at worst) tolerated, but (at best) liked and certainly trusted by the other characters. After some of Iago's fooling, Cassio amusedly tells Desdemona that Iago 'speaks home' and that 'you may relish him more in the soldier than in the scholar' (II, i, 165–6). In similar tolerant amusement, Pompey urges Enobarbus to 'Enjoy thy plainness, It nothing ill becomes thee' (II, vi). What is most interesting is audience-reaction to the two characters, as the roles are acted out within two quite different plays. Enobarbus's plain-speaking is a constant source of delight: his mockery has a sharp edge, but it has also gaiety and good humour, and his camaraderie is the expression of an open nature. On the other hand, any audience watching Iago's attempts at clowning will feel repelled, being always aware of the malevolent nature behind the mask. And indeed Shakespeare ensures that we do feel this way: Cassio has just finished speaking (above), or perhaps he is still speaking, when we hear Iago gloating, aside, that 'as little a web as this will ensnare as great a fly as Cassio'. In Iago Shakespeare created a sour and malevolent version of the honest soldier he was to show so delightfully in Enobarbus. The latter's loyalty to his general (which the audience never doubts) is expressed in the plain-speaking through which he tries to force Antony to see military matters realistically and to act in a way worthy of himself. The audience suffers with him through his eventual betrayal of Antony, who reacts with characteristic generosity: 'O, my fortunes have corrupted honest men' (IV, v). 'Honest' Enobarbus *is*, although this is the only time the word is applied to him; in the next scene his heart cracks as he thinks of his betrayal of his general. Iago aims always to bring his general down; and he eventually does so (to despair, grief, degradation, and murder) by trading upon his reputation for being what Enobarbus *is*.

'Honest Iago'

Every student of language and literature, but more especially every student of Shakespeare's Iago, is indebted to William Empson for his brilliant elucidation of some of the complexities of the word 'honest'. He calls it 'a very queer business' that Shakespeare should seem almost obsessed in *Othello*, with its many shades of meaning. Empson writes:

> . . . the word was in the middle of a rather complicated process of change and [what] emerged from it was a sort of jovial cult of independence . . . it came to have in it a covert assertion that the man who accepts the natural desires, who does not live by principle, will be fit for such warm uses of honest as imply 'generous' and 'faithful to friends' or employers.

There was often something a little patronising in its use; it carried 'an obscure social insult as well as a hint of stupidity'.[6]

There is much in this and in many of Empson's other points which illuminates the way Iago is seen by others within the play, the way he sees things, and the way he works.

For instance, his 'Whip me these honest knaves' places exactly his own view: to him a Kent or an Enobarbus would be a fool, a mere 'duteous and knee-crooking knave . . . doting on his own obsequious bondage' (I, i, 45, 46, 49). To Iago all such men *must* be simply insincere time-servers; he believes that only 'shows of service' matter. Recalling this, the audience will feel the ominous irony when (and this is the next time the word is used in the play) Othello buttresses it with a stronger word when he assures the Duke 'A man he is of honesty and trust', and soon after addresses him as 'Honest Iago' (I, iii, 284, 294).

Empson emphasises the frequent, varied, and of course deliberate ambiguities in the word in *Othello*. When Iago says Othello 'thinks men honest', he means Othello thinks them both trustworthy and truthful. This suggests a quality in Othello himself which is very much like another sort of honesty pinpointed by Empson. '. . . "honest Tom at the fair" is going to be cheated . . .':[7] to be honest in this way may mean to be 'simple', 'easily deceived'. Ambiguity of a different sort comes into Iago's 'As honest as I am' (II, i, 201): partly there is the patronising sense, for Iago means 'Slightly looked down on as I am'; partly he means again trustworthy, and is referring sarcastically to his supposed faithfulness.

Montano tells Iago 'It were an honest action to say so/To the Moor' (II, iii, 134–5): Iago would be faithful to his position of trust with Othello

---

[6] *The Structure of Complex Words*, p. 218. The book has three chapters on the word 'honest', the third dealing specifically with its uses in *Othello*.
[7] Op. cit., p. 210.

if he spoke the truth about Cassio's supposed drunkenness. Exactly these meanings come into a later exchange even though the word 'honest' does not occur: Montano urges Iago not to let honesty (faithfulness to friends—Cassio) outweigh the obligation to be honest (faithful to Othello and truthful about Cassio's weakness) (II, iii, 209–11). Later Iago is made to play on the word when Cassio thanks him for his advice and Iago protests 'in the sincerity of love and honest kindness': both faithfulness and truth-telling are implicit (II, iii, 319). A little later he soliloquises: it is easy to win Desdemona 'in any honest suit'. Here he uses the word 'straight', for what he says is true and in line with what he has told Cassio. The irony, for the audience, lies in the way he uses truth for an evil end. The effect on the victim is evident: Cassio has complete confidence in, precisely, Iago's faithfulness to friends. Just after his disgrace, he is sure he has 'well approv'd' Iago's love for him (II, iii, 303); he has never known 'A Florentine more kind and honest' (III, i, 40–1).

In the temptation of Othello, the secret of Iago's success is that he makes it seem that Othello's honest (faithful, reliable) ancient is at first too honest (faithful to his friend, Cassio) to be honest (tell the truth) about what is in his mind. Othello's trust in Cassio's reliability has already been shaken, so he is the more open to further distrust of his honesty (in other ways). After Iago has come to speak more 'frankly', it appears to Othello that now Iago has let loyalty to Othello outweigh loyalty to Cassio: further, it seems to him that since this faithful and reliable creature has had to be so urged to speak out, what he says (out of loyalty and so much against his will) must be true.

Another sense of honesty comes in when Iago says it would not be for his 'manhood, honesty, or wisdom' to speak his thoughts. Empson takes this to be a sort of propriety, a meaning close to the use of honesty to mean chastity in women. This is often used of Desdemona. The sad irony is that Desdemona's one small lapse in honesty (truth-telling) leads Othello to doubt much further her honesty (chastity). Even sadder, this has come about through his trust in the false Iago. He gradually comes to believe in Desdemona's falsity, moving from the first suspicion 'I do not doubt but Desdemona's honest' to the savagery of 'false as hell' in the brothel scene. The corrective comes only after she has been 'falsely, falsely murder'd', after Emilia's incredulous 'She false?' Iago through his own falsity (which seems always the opposite) has brought Othello to see Desdemona's honesty as falsity.

How does Iago work? His power to manipulate people comes from his insight, not only into their weaknesses, but into their good qualities. He sees what they are, and plays unfeelingly on good points and weaknesses alike. Often he lies, but often gains his ends by actually telling the truth. His first idea for his plot comes from his knowledge of Desdemona's goodness, and his advice to Cassio is based on it. He has told Roderigo that Desdemona is *not* 'of most blest condition', but his truth-telling can often be tested by his purpose. He wants Cassio to appeal to Desdemona's goodness; he wants Roderigo to think her light and fickle. An interesting instance of his telling the truth occurs when he speaks to Desdemona, Emilia, and Cassio at the moment when, on his prompting, Cassio has just come to beg Desdemona to intercede again for him with Othello. Othello's anger is worrying all three, and Iago asks 'Is my lord angry?'; his picture of Othello, unmoved in battle, is doubtless a true one (III, iv, 131–6). It fits well with Lodovico's 'Is this . . . the noble nature/ Whom passion could not shake?' (IV, i, 260–62). To speak truth at this point suits Iago's purpose, which is to cover himself by appearing to share the the deep concern which the others are feeling. This is a case where, on the stage, the actor must sound genuinely concerned; for the audience, knowing his true nature, this will highlight the falsity.

When Iago speaks cynically of 'love' as lust, asserting confidently that Othello and Desdemona must soon feel satiety, and that Cassio must be passionately in love with Desdemona and wish to win her favours, the situation is more complicated. Probably he believes what he says. But when he speaks in this way to others he has an obvious motive, and he later seems to contradict himself. In soliloquy he tells us (and we will certainly feel it to be true) that Othello is

> of a constant, noble, loving nature
> And I dare think he'll prove to Desdemona
> A most dear husband. (II, i, 284–6)

Which, to Iago, is the truth? For a possible resolution of the problem, see Appendix D, p. 67.

In manipulating Othello, Iago makes good use of his knowledge of the man. One of Othello's weaknesses is a part of his essential goodness, but to Iago it is useful. When he first plans to 'abuse Othello's ear', he muses:

> The Moor a free and open nature, too,
> That thinks men honest that but seem to be so. (I, iii, 397–8)

It is on this basis that he sets about leading him by the nose 'as tenderly as asses are'. It is not quite so easy as that, as the next chapter will attempt to show.

5. Othello's Nature and the Tragedy

The Brawl Scene

Although Iago does not make the tragedy out of nothing, it is a serious mistake to go to the other extreme and see him as 'merely ancillary'.[1] This is to ignore the inseparable relationship of victim and torturer and to give too much weight to Othello's faults.

One of Othello's weaknesses, perhaps the chief (though superficially not very serious), is clearly and economically shown in the brawl scene (II, iii). The brawl itself is entirely stage-managed by Iago, and in the course of it he acts his numerous parts with the greatest skill and enjoyment. Before it begins we have watched him set on his dupe, Roderigo, to make trouble with Cassio; now he sings and plays the good fellow as he induces Cassio to drink; he lies to Montano about Cassio's 'infirmity'; he orders Roderigo to further action; he pretends to be deeply concerned and to try to restrain Cassio as Othello appears; he finally acts the part, for Othello and everyone else, of 'Honest Iago, that look'st dead with grieving'. Watching what Granville Barker calls the 'chameleon-like ability of Iago', the audience should feel his tremendous energy and quick adaption to each change in the situation. Into the turmoil comes Othello, very much the noble Moor of whom Montano has just been speaking. His manner is stern, commanding, but unmoved by passion. It is only after Iago, Cassio, and the wounded Montano have all refused to answer his 'What is the matter, masters?', that his passion rises, and having darkened his judgement (as he recognises himself) 'assays to lead the way. . .'. Othello sees the brawl as a 'monstrous' offence, a breach of trust, and demands: 'Iago, who began't?' At this (virtually a command) Iago still pretends to hesitate, and Montano has to urge him, before he

[1] F. R. Leavis, *The Common Pursuit*, p. 138.

tells his story with the greatest possible show of reluctance to testify against Cassio. This, with his studied efforts to excuse his friend, prompts Othello's

> I know, Iago,
> Thy honesty and love doth mince this matter
> Making it light to Cassio. (II, iii, 237–9)

This is a crucial point, for here Shakespeare shows, precisely, an element basic to Othello's trust in Iago. At the same time the scene shows something within Othello's nature which is equally crucial to the tragedy. Now that he is certain (on Iago's evidence, which he cannot know to be false) he quickly and authoritatively, but once again without a trace of passion, cashiers Cassio, then turns with tenderness to 'my gentle love', deals calmly and quickly with the remaining details of the affray, and retires with a near-joke to Desdemona.

Shakespeare expanded a single sentence from Cinthio[2] to a scene of considerable length, obviously with the serious dramatic purpose of showing some of the forces which contribute to the tragedy. It is evident that Othello's passion rises here only because of his uncertainty. He is responsible for administering justice and enforcing discipline: he must and will know who is responsible. He must and will act. This crucial characteristic is one on which we later see Iago work deliberately; it is the root of Othello's being 'perplex'd in the extreme'. If we glance ahead to the temptation, a key speech becomes very ominous in the later context:

> Think'st thou I'd make a life of jealousy?
> . . . No, to be once in doubt,
> Is once to be resolv'd . . . (III, iii, 181, 183–4)

Further, and this too is crucial, once he is certain, Othello acts quietly and firmly. He cashiers Cassio in the conviction that it is both necessary to military discipline and quite just, and he is therefore able to do it in spite of his own personal affection for Cassio. This is a scene in which the

---

[2] Cf. Furness *Variorum*, p. 379 (I prefer to translate the italicised phrase by 'while on guard'):

Et non passò molto, che il Moro, per haver messa mano alla spada il Capo di squadra, *nella guardia*, contra un soldato, e dategli delle ferite, lo privò del grado . . .

Not long afterwards, it happened that the Captain, having drawn his sword upon a soldier *of the guard*, and struck him, the Moor deprived him of his rank . . .

stage presentation should be revealing. When Othello first comes in, it
should be felt that a large and commanding presence is dominating the
confusion which we have watched Iago engineer. Then, after his passionate outburst, Othello should be very calm, though firm. The audience
should feel that he means it when he speaks of his affection for 'Cassio',
miss the intimacy of the former 'Michael', and also feel his determination
to act justly, whoever is involved, for he has already threatened to punish
the culprit 'though he had twinn'd with me at a birth'.

To understand the tragedy, it is crucial to see how all this has come
about: through Iago's diabolically clever 'frame-up'. His plot has been so
successful as to reduce Cassio to a state of silent shame, with no will to
speak in his own defence. He, as much as Othello, Montano, and all the
others, believe in his guilt and in both the reluctance and reliability of
Iago's evidence against him. Iago has most effectively consolidated
everyone's absolute belief in his 'honesty'—in all senses of the word.

In this scene, then, Shakespeare shows a terrible foreshadowing of
Othello's later reactions. 'Perplex'd', he will be incapable of calm and
decisive action; compelled by his nature to act, he will not be able to
act calmly as he eventually does here. He will be prey to agonising
sexual jealousy when Iago's later plot has at the same time deliberately
aroused this and fostered a confused sense that Desdemona's 'iniquity'
demands a terrible justice—hence his murderous vengeance. When he
finds out the truth, his final act of justice is to take his own life. In all
three situations he is convinced he is administering justice, and does
so despite personal feelings: first on Cassio, who is not only his trusted
subordinate but his friend; then on Desdemona whom he loves deeply;
finally on himself. Iago's 'practice' leads him from the first to the second
of these tragically mistaken acts, and, inevitably, to the last.

The brawl scene is most noteworthy for the way Shakespeare shows
Iago's manipulation of people: even before the actual brawl, the audience
sees him at work on Montano, winning him in advance to belief in
Cassio's 'engrafted infirmity', so that it is Montano who in the end
appears to have to persuade Iago that he is 'no soldier' if he does not tell
'the truth'. This means that Montano, Othello, and everyone else are
convinced that Iago, having first tried to shield Cassio altogether, is trying at least to find excuses for his friend. The parallel with Iago's later
tactics with Othello is obvious. Indeed, this is what makes it possible to
understand precisely what causes the first movement of suspicion in
Othello. When Iago has protested that he loves Othello, Othello replies:

I think thou dost,
And for I know thou art full of love and honesty
And weighest thy words, before thou give 'em breath,
Therefore these stops of thine fright me the more: ...

(III, iii, 121–4)

Othello is, therefore, no mere naïve, self-esteeming dupe: he has no reason for distrusting Iago, nor has anyone else within the play—with the interesting exception of Roderigo, who is a Shakespearean innovation, created as a contrast to Othello. For Roderigo is a thorough-going dupe, the only person who knows enough of Iago's true nature to suspect him, yet continues to allow himself to be gulled.

The Quality of Othello's Love

Here we must consider a fairly widely held view: that, clever as Iago's plotting is, 'Othello believes a person whom he does not love or really know and has no right reason to trust, to the point of disbelieving persons whom he loves and has every reason to trust'.[3] Othello has complete confidence in Iago when he entrusts Desdemona to his care, and, in fact, appears to know him well. His faith in him is based partly on the deep bond which grows between officers and their trusted subordinates—strengthened by Iago's various protestations and by every detail of his behaviour in the brawl scene.

Othello certainly loves Desdemona, but there is no textual ground for maintaining that he has every reason to trust her. To the audience, she is clearly trustworthy because the audience is plainly shown her fidelity in ways that Othello is not. Herein lies part of the tragedy: Othello does not really know his wife. Othello and Desdemona are among the most touching of literature's lovers because we have the impression that neither knows the other very well. F. R. Leavis calls Professor Bradley 'comically innocent' for expressing the view that 'Othello really knows nothing about his wife'.[4] For a start, that is not what Bradley says: he says 'in the circumstances he cannot have known much of Desdemona before his marriage', and speaks of Othello's 'utter powerlessness to repel it [Iago's insinuation] on the ground of knowledge of his wife'.[5] It is critically fashionable to decry Bradley for his psychologising about characters as if they were real people, but there are still things to be

---

[3] E. E. Stoll, *Art and Artifice in Shakespeare*, p. 7.
[4] *The Common Pursuit*, p. 141.   [5] *Shakespearean Tragedy*, p. 157.

learned from his insights. Where in the text do we have the smallest evidence that Othello does know her well? Or that he has had time to do so? In Cinthio the couple have ample time to get to know each other before the events of the tragedy. In Shakespeare's play they do not. Did Shakespeare make such a significant change by mere inadvertence?

Closely related to this and to the course of the tragedy is the quality of Othello's love. The incantatory beauty of the 'Othello music' (Wilson Knight's phrase) reinforces our conviction that Shakespeare meant to retain from Cinthio the idea of this marriage as a spiritual union.[6] Othello's language soars to the peak of beauty and emotion when the pair are reunited in Cyprus. The worth of this love, his 'wonder' at his own absolute 'content' are touchingly apparent. The words are especially revealing since to Iago Othello has expressed something of his reluctance to commit himself to love at all; love is something wonderful and new to him, for which he has finally given up his 'unhous'd free condition'.

This in turn has a close bearing on an aspect of Othello's love to which Robert Speaight refers when he speculates on the possible effects on Othello of the consummation of his marriage.[7] It would be ridiculous to try to look back into Othello's past and to try to determine what his previous experience of love has been, but the text shows that it is his adventures and battles which have been his passion. Iago calls him the 'lusty Moor' and Roderigo 'the lascivious Moor', but their evidence is unreliable in itself and completely unsupported. Othello's own claim is that he is old enough no longer to feel 'the young affects of passion'. He says this before his wedding night, and doubtless he is wrong; but the evidence suggests that he genuinely thinks of himself in this way, because prior to his marriage sexual experience does not seem very important to him. The tender idealistic qualities of any love (so apparent in Othello's) are sure to be deepened by sensual love: certainly the

[6] Cf. Furness *Variorum*, p. 377 (Furness omits from his translation the crucial phrase—in square brackets below): 'Avenne che una virtuosa Donna, di maravigliosa bellezza, Disdemona chiamata, tratta [non di appetito donnesco ma] dalla virtù del Moro, s'innamorò di lui: et egli, vinto dalla bellezza et dal nobile *pensiero* della Donna, similmente di lei si accese . . .'
It happened that a virtuous lady of great beauty, named Disdemona, fell in love with the Moor, moved thereto [not by feminine appetite but] by his valour: and he, vanquished by the beauty and the noble *character* of the lady, returned her love . . . (I prefer to translate the italicised word by 'mind' rather than by Furness's 'character'.)

[7] *Nature in Shakespearian Tragedy*, pp. 75–8.

dimension added (although it may seldom in itself cause jealousy) is likely to intensify it if jealousy should otherwise arise. If this is relevant to Othello's case, as seems likely, it adds another element of vulnerability. The language confirms the point: it certainly eliminates the possibility that Othello is shocked in any unpleasant sense by the revelation of his wife's sensuality (Desdemona 'did love the Moor to live with him'; she is a whole woman, not an ice maiden). Immediately after the wedding night, we see Othello uxoriously assuring Desdemona that he can deny her nothing, and expressing his love in the beauty of:

> Excellent wretch, perdition catch my soul
> But I do love thee, and when I love thee not,
> Chaos is come again. (III, iii, 91–3)

In the period of Othello's jealousy and murderous passion, the sharply sensual language repeatedly associated with Desdemona has often been noted. It contains many images of taste and smell, such language as to suggest an almost unbearable sweetness of the sort associated with the most intense sensual delight. In his jealousy the images are either inverted, or perverted to the sexually loathsome, or juxtaposed with images of foulness and corruption. Leavis assesses Othello's love as 'more self-centred and self-regarding satisfaction—pride, sensual possessiveness, appetite, love of loving than he . . . suspects.'[8] Leaving aside the fact that most human love mingles any or all of these with its finer elements, this simply does not go with the sort of poetry associated with Othello's love. Caroline Spurgeon speaks of the 'exquisitely tuned music of Othello's joy'.[9] In this music we see nothing of the sort of hollow, self-deceiving, self-dramatising language which Shakespeare matches very well with some of his lovers (cf. Appendix D).

The quality of Othello's love is not to be judged by the destructive passion which is a terrible and temporary perversion of it. It is relevant, too, to note the extent to which tenderness breaks into Othello's speech again and again even after he has decided upon his murderous justice, although it is almost always coupled with a longing which is plainly sensual. Among many examples of recurring tenderness in moods of vengeful rage, perhaps the most poignant comes in the terrible brothel scene, breaking through in these beautiful lines:

> Yet could I bear that too, well, very well:
> But there, where I have garner'd up my heart,

[8] *The Common Pursuit*, p. 141.   [9] *Shakespeare's Imagery*, p. 70.

Where either I must live, or bear no life,
The fountain, from the which my current runs,
Or else dries up, to be discarded thence . . . (IV, ii, 57–61)

The flow of this comes as a lovely echo of the earlier music of Othello's
joy and speaks eloquently in words associated with the richness and
fruition of a happy love: there is the phrase 'garner'd up my heart' with
its connotation of the storing up of something of great worth; the
'fountain' suggests love as the pure and essential source of Othello's life;
the 'to be discarded thence' brings to the audience the essence of his
agony, confirming Bradley's contention that what Othello mistakenly
mourns is 'the wreck of his faith and love',[10] its corruption. This is borne
out by the foulness of the imagery which immediately follows (of toads
breeding in a cistern). Sometimes the lines preceding those above are
quoted in an attempt to show that what Othello cannot bear is to be a
figure of scorn. At several points it is evident that Othello feels the shame
of being a cuckold, but the solemnity and beauty of the poetry in which
he expresses his real grief can leave no doubt as to which Shakespeare
meant to be over-riding.

The Othello we see, in the text and on the stage, is newly married,
middle-aged, his love a combination of idealising worship (not yet based
on real knowledge of his wife) and of newly-roused passion—thus
especially vulnerable to Iago's convincing suggestions of Desdemona's
infidelity.

A final point is necessary here, but only because of Leavis's contention
that the tragedy is 'inherent in the Othello-Desdemona relationship'.[11]
It would be most improper to speculate about *what does not happen* in
Shakespeare's play, if Leavis's phrase did not imply that even without
Iago, tragedy would have come about. The text, however, shows no
'mechanism', internal or external, strong enough to bring tragedy into
this happy marriage—except Iago. And it is the language which makes
the point. The language will not, for instance allow us to accept that
there *is* anything 'unnatural' in the marriage, as Brabantio insists ('for
nature so preposterously to err'; 'Against all rules of nature'; I, iii, 62,
101), echoed by Othello's own words (III, iii, 231) which are taken
up at once by Iago. Both Roderigo and Iago speak grossly of 'the
Moor' and his blackness, but Roderigo's jealousy is probably heightened
by prejudice, and Iago speaks from his own base nature and baser

[10] *Shakespearean Tragedy*, p. 158.   [11] *The Common Pursuit*, p. 141.

motives. No one else expresses such views; and what counts most is the nature of each of the two people concerned. Both are said to be free, open, generous, and noble or blessed in 'nature', and are shown to be so. Desdemona sees 'Othello's visage in his mind'; Othello wants her to be with him so he can be 'free and bounteous of her mind'.

What *is* unnatural is the 'death . . . that kills for loving', as Desdemona says (V, ii, 42)—that is, the vengeful 'monster' of jealousy in Othello's mind. This is not a monster 'begot upon itself' (in Emilia's words, III, iv, 159–60) but 'engendr'd' by Iago's 'poison'. The 'monstrous birth' to which he looks forward gloatingly (I, iii, 402) is the birth of Othello's jealousy; this is where nature does indeed preposterously err from itself— for Othello's is not at all a jealous nature.

The 'gentle' and loving Desdemona's hero-worship, her sensuality, and her qualities of mind are exactly the qualities to make Othello happy. Her absolute ideal of fidelity, her dying words, in which she tries to shift the blame for the monstrous deed to herself, her commending herself to 'my kind lord', all testify to the quality of her love. Many of Othello's words have been seen to testify to the quality of his, not least those uttered when he still suffers from the anguished conviction of his wife's falsity:

> . . . nay had she been true,
> If heaven would make me such another world
> Of one entire and perfect chrysolite
> I'ld not have sold her for it. (V, ii, 144–7)

The undoubted value of this marriage is established in the words of the text. Despite vast dissimilarities of background, and all their superficial unlikenesses, Desdemona and Othello are kindred natures. The tragedy of *Othello* lies not only in the horror of the storm which sweeps Othello himself, but in the tragic waste brought about when the Desdemona-Othello relationship is destroyed (*cf.* Appendix D, p. 67).

Othello's Simplicity and Nobility

Othello is simple in several ways. Iago's evidence (I, iii, 397) can be accepted, because it is precisely on his victim's trusting nature that he goes to work. Iago's words (II, i, 283–6) about Othello's nobility and goodness can be taken as true, too, because he is grudgingly acknowledging qualities in Othello in spite of his hatred for him; furthermore they highlight his own evil desire to attack this goodness. Othello's nobility is further attested by many references to it and by the respect in which he is universally held.

Part of this arises from his being a simple and direct man of action with a simple direct approach to the demands of his position. With this goes his simple natural air of authority. Shakespeare establishes this not only in the brawl scene, but most painstakingly in the other early scenes of the play, thus disposing of any contention that Othello is given to self-dramatisation and self-idealisation. We simply do not see these qualities in his manner of dealing with disturbances which would have afforded perfect opportunities if Shakespeare had wished to show Othello in this light. What, in fact, he shows in great detail is *the precise opposite*.

It is most significant, for instance, that the first words Othello speaks in the play are his quiet 'Tis better as it is' (I, ii, 6). They are in reply to Iago, who is busily protesting that he has scarcely been able to restrain himself when Othello has been spoken of in 'scurvy' and 'provoking' terms; and they should come with great force to the audience, for Iago has just been giving a picture of Othello as bombastic and 'loving his own pride and purpose'. Now, seeing Othello, we should see no wounded self-esteem in his manner (Iago is on the wrong track here), and in the rest of this scene his behaviour is wholly in keeping with the first impression. It is a model of quiet dignity, quiet confidence, quiet readiness to meet Brabantio or anyone else, despite Iago's renewed efforts to stir things up. The tragedy of *Othello* is that a *man like this*, can be 'wrought' to such savage behaviour; if he is not a man like this, the tragedy, if it does not disappear altogether, becomes much less moving. Much can be made of this on the stage. The audience should feel immediately something of the tremendous contrast between the natures of the two men. We have just seen Iago in characteristic action; if, in this scene with Othello, he does not actually move about much, he should give the impression of physical and nervous energy, while Othello should convey, through bearing, manner, and dignity of movement, a kind of inner stillness. Iago's complete failure here to rouse Othello to anger or to action should make a comment about both characters.

The same quiet dignity becomes even more impressive in the face of the growing provocation to which Othello is subjected. When the enraged Brabantio comes in with his retinue, swords down, Othello responds with unruffled courtesy. More revealing still is his response to a most insulting and sustained verbal attack from Brabantio, which ends with an order to his men to 'Lay hold on' Othello, and with the direct threat 'If he do resist/Subdue him at his peril'. Othello's quiet reply entirely bears out his previous claim that 'My parts, title and my perfect soul/Shall manifest me rightly'. It would be impossible to imagine any behaviour further removed from undue pride in himself, exhibitionism, self-dramatisation. Yet we are asked by Leavis and other critics to accept that these are characteristic of Othello and central to his downfall. At the beginning of the play, Shakespeare shows Othello when he is neither 'wrought' nor 'perplex'd'—in his true simplicity and nobility. This must be of supreme importance to understanding the character, for it is repeatedly established here: the same impressively unruffled serenity and quiet confidence is maintained throughout the scene in which he answers Brabantio's insulting accusations. Othello's manner must be imagined, once again, through the beauty of his words. Any pompous, self-glorifying delivery in the story of his wooing would be entirely at variance with the words, as was a recent film interpretation in which the account ended with a knowing leer and a wink after the line: 'This only is the witch-craft I have used.' This must devalue the tragedy by devaluing the worth of the man whose tragedy it is. When Othello speaks the above line with quiet, almost solemn, sincerity, the audience should be half spell-bound and feel with the Duke, 'I think this tale would win my daughter too . . .'.

Within Othello's very simplicity, admirable as it is, are qualities which make him vulnerable.

Not far below the unruffled surface are passions of which he is himself, doubtless, unaware. This is not to say that he is a simple savage with primitive passions ready to erupt easily; but there is a quality in his jealous rage, once aroused, which is savage, almost primitive in its ferocity. This is linked closely with his inability to pause and reflect or to remain in doubt. At the end of the play, Lodovico calls him 'this *rash* and most unfortunate man' (my italics).

Othello feels a kind of naïve wonder at his experiences and his dangers, a wonder that Desdemona shares; he wonders at his own life and at Desdemona's having loved him for his dangers; above all he wonders at their love and his own contentment. Wonder is a beautiful, childlike quality, harmless, even endearing, but it adds to his vulnerability for it seems to him almost too good to be true that Desdemona should really love him (*cf.* p. 54). Wonder is linked too with a touch of superstition in Othello's nature, beautifully and tragically linked in such a way as to invest the fatal handkerchief with special importance and value to him. The significance of this can be seen in the context of an analysis of the course of Iago's temptation and sustained manipulation of Othello.

How It Is Done

'Ha, I like not that.' Thus Iago begins his concentrated attack on Othello's faith in his wife, an attack which will continue in a pattern of advances, feigned retreats, adaptations, until he succeeds. Adaptation is the key word, for it is the flexibility of Iago's responses to the responses of his prey that is wonderful in the subtlety of detail with which Shakespeare presents it.

Iago's remark comes just as Cassio goes out. A man jealous by nature would need no more than that—Leontes, with his 'diseas'd opinion', less (*cf.* Appendix C). A jealous man would certainly notice enough to be alert to Iago's next 'Nothing, my lord, or if . . . I know not what'; not to mention the plain hint in:

> Cassio, my lord?. . . no, sure, I cannot think it,
> That he would sneak away so guilty-like,
> Seeing you coming. (III, iii, 39-41)

All this appears to have not the slightest effect on Othello, for as Desdemona goes out he muses on his love. Iago has to begin again, his manner strongly suggestive of some 'harm' beyond the mere 'satisfaction of my thought.' His deliberately needling repetition of Othello's words ('Indeed?'; 'Honest, my lord?'; 'Think, my lord?') quickly gives Othello the idea that he is hiding something. Bearing in mind the brawl scene, the audience should understand immediately Othello's disquiet. Iago proceeds by sustained insinuation aimed at strengthening Othello's impression that he is hiding something, so it is not surprising that Othello is soon crying 'By heaven, I'll know your thought'. Iago's 'You cannot' is calculated to inflame further; then comes some revelation of the 'thought' he is so carefully 'hiding', with the warning against 'jealousy'. The text gives no certainty but if, as seems likely, Othello's suspicions have first turned only to Cassio, he must at this stage begin to associate Desdemona with the implications, especially when Iago makes bold to use the word 'cuckold'. Othello's 'O misery' brings pious words of advice from Iago, followed by Othello's firm declaration that he will not lead a life dominated by continuing and unresolved suspicion. He outlines exactly the course he will try to follow—and which indeed we watch him try to follow:

> . . . No, Iago,
> I'll see before I doubt, when I doubt, prove,
> And on the proof, there is no more but this:
> Away at once with love or jealousy! (III, iii, 193–6)

Iago, 'glad of it', is emboldened to speak more freely. The suggestiveness of 'I speak not *yet* of proof' (my italics) he follows with advice which goes counter to Othello's nature, and of course is calculated as such: 'Wear your eye thus not jealous nor secure'—that is, remain in doubt. Leavis explains Othello's 'immediate surrender' (but Othello has not yet surrendered) in terms of what comes next, claiming that what Othello succumbs to is an appeal to his 'ideal conception of himself'[12] (in Iago's 'I would not have your free and noble nature/Out of self-bounty be abused'). From textual evidence so far, it is quite inconsistent to suppose that Othello will suddenly be moved by an appeal to self-esteem; but from textual evidence there is every reason to expect him to react unfavourably to any suggestion that he should continue in doubt. Iago goes on in such a way as to strengthen the doubt. Then comes an instance where the social background is a crucial element in the tragedy, making Othello uncertain, insecure, therefore more vulnerable. Othello *is* an alien, and there is reason for him to take note when Iago, who does 'know our country disposition well', warns him that feminine infidelity is simply an accepted Venetian custom. From this Iago cleverly moves straight on to a point which Othello knows to be a fact. He refers to Desdemona's deception of her father (directly echoing Brabantio's earlier warning at I, iii, 292–3), pressing the point and adding a further clever twist. It was, he suggests, Desdemona's unusual *skill* in deception, the fact that 'She . . . so young could give out such a seeming' which made her father think she must have been bewitched.

After these very telling points, Iago's skill in 'playing' his victim is shown in his drawing back, as it were, saying that he is 'to blame' for loving Othello too well. Othello's 'I am bound to you forever' stresses (with its terrible irony) his fatal trust; the sombre tone of it may be deduced from Iago's 'I see this hath a little dashed your spirits', from Othello's 'O, not a jot; not a jot', from Iago's 'But I do see you're moved'. In mock reassurance he again gives Othello the impossible

---

[12] *The Common Pursuit*, pp. 140, 145.

advice not to go any further than 'suspicion'; then protests 'Cassio's my worthy friend', recalling inevitably the brawl scene. Doubtless this is why Othello is both worried and perplexed, and showing it, for, for the third time, Iago comments with mock concern 'My lord, I see you're moved'. To Othello's 'No, not much moved/I do not think but Desdemona's honest' comes again the calculated insinuation in '. . . long live you to think so', which brings Othello's unhappy speculation 'and yet how nature erring from itself'. This is seized upon by Iago. He 'fears' she may indeed 'repent' after comparing Othello unfavourably with 'her country forms'. Iago leaves at Othello's request, and Othello, much disturbed, sighs, 'Why did I marry?' Leavis not only attributes Iago's success to his having successfully appealed to Othello's 'self-idealisation', but worse, he refers back to Iago's words (at I, i, 12) as proving that Othello *does* love 'his own pride and purposes'. This is to go straight against what the text so plainly shows, and against what comes next: Othello's next words reaffirm what *has* brought him to this sad state of agonising doubt:

> This honest creature doubtless
> Sees and knows more, much more than he unfolds. (III, iii, 246–7)

This is precisely the impression the audience has watched Iago create, and explains the extent to which Othello is now moved. To regard Iago as 'merely ancillary', 'a mechanism necessary for precipitating tragedy'[13] (another would have done as well?), is to under-rate very seriously Shakespeare's artistry in showing the subtlety of Iago's machinations within a tragic pattern which is very complex indeed.

At this point, for example, Iago knows that Othello is deeply disturbed. He knows Othello's nature, that he must and will be resolved of doubt. What does he do? He returns again to 'entreat' Othello with an air of great concern to 'Leave it to time'.

Now Othello's torment begins in earnest. His next speech contains disconnected elements expressive of conflict. The music is 'untuned': he reiterates his confidence in Iago, threatens vengeance; then on a quieter note speculates on his own 'demerits', without, however, dwelling on these or giving any indication of injured self-esteem; and ends with a despairing outburst: 'She's gone; I am abused.' His torment is complex: if Desdemona is false, he must hate her and take a just revenge; since Iago seems to know so much more than he will reveal, it seems likely that she is false. This is the way Othello sees it; yet his love and his desire continue

[13] *The Common Pursuit*, p. 141.

to battle against any real conviction that she is false. This is what gives to all the succeeding scenes of the play their peculiarly painful quality. Seeing Desdemona as she comes in, he is unable to believe her false; he is so moved that he can hardly speak.

Iago is next seen gloating over the working of his 'poison'; and he now possesses the handkerchief, which, he thinks, 'may do something'. Othello, 'on the rack', feels in his bewilderment and uncertainty, that anything would be preferable to doubt. Deprived of his 'tranquil mind', and his 'content', even his 'occupation', in which he has taken great pride and satisfaction, means nothing. Here, his passion roused, he becomes temporarily rhetorical, self-dramatising; he is certainly falsifying his real feelings in his wild assertion that it would have been better, he would have been happier, however Desdemona had behaved, 'So I had nothing known', for the mere thought of her falsity is then so intolerable that he turns savagely on Iago and demands 'ocular proof'. His hands upon Iago's throat, his terrible speech:

> If thou dost slander her and torture me
> Never pray more; abandon all remorse; (III, iii, 374–5)

awakens a response in Iago which is typical in its flexible adjustment to the unexpected. This is a very bad moment for Iago: not only may his scheme fail, but he knows Othello well enough to know where Othello's vengeance will strike if he is found out. It is probably less fear for his skin than sheer skill and zest in playing his terrible game which prompts him to turn Othello's 'waked wrath', as nothing else could have done, by a show of offended innocence. This so throws Othello back into perplexity that it is painful to see:

>   By the world,
> I think my wife be honest, and think she is not,
> I think that thou art just, and think thou art not;
> I'll have some proof: her name, that was as fresh
> As Dian's visage, is now begrim'd, and black
> As mine own face:
>   . . . would I were satisfied! (III, iii, 389–94, 396)

Here I replace F's 'my name'—in the 1958 Arden *Othello*—with Q2's 'her name'. On the basis of meaning in the context, 'her' is clearly preferable. The speech comes in the context of Othello's rage against Iago, to whom he has just said 'If thou does slander *her* . . .'; and in the beginning of the speech it is his wife's honour he is talking about; there is nothing else in all this about his own honour. Furthermore, the actual construction makes 'her name' a more fitting contrast with 'mine own face'. It is also more fitting that 'her name' should be compared with Diana's face; the goddess of chastity is a fine contrast to the slur on Desdemona's honour, and is a reminder of her real purity.

'Eaten up with passion', Othello 'would' and 'will' be satisfied. Iago, more desperate, becomes bolder, and his speech becomes correspondingly more grossly suggestive. The picture which he suggests of the adulterous pair is vividly and coarsely drawn: 'Would you grossly gape on— behold her topp'd?' Iago goes on to press this point, implying the adultery as a fact, the only difficulty being to 'bring them to that prospect', hot as their passions may be, gross fools as they may be (but with the insinuation that they are far from fools in such matters). Then he offers 'satisfaction' on the basis of strong circumstantial evidence. To Othello's 'Give me a living reason she's disloyal', Iago, with a show of distaste, tells of Cassio's supposed dream, again picturing such details as to wring from Othello 'O, monstrous, monstrous'. Iago's subtlety is then apparent as he says '. . . this was but his dream . . .', knowing that the details will have affected the victim so strongly that Iago can afford to say this and then immediately come round and appear to admit that it could 'help to thicken *other proofs*' (my italics).

The Handkerchief

Here, for the first time, comes in the handkerchief, which from now on will be vital to the course of the tragedy. Typically, Iago, feeling his way, brings it in when he appears to be trying to comfort and pacify Othello:

> Nay but be wise yet we see nothing done,
> She may be honest yet; tell me but this, (III, iii, 439–40)

with then a question about the handkerchief, and the gross picture of the use Cassio has made of it. Othello's 'If it be that . . .' suggests some of the significance of the particular handkerchief; and, smarting from the suggestion of the way in which Cassio has used his first gift to his wife, he declares 'Now I do see 'tis true'. Love is 'gone', and a just vengeance is invoked. There is the cold horror of his likening his 'bloody thoughts' to the 'icy current and compulsive course' of the Pontic sea. There is the travesty of a religious or knightly oath. It is Iago (now his 'lieutenant') who says 'I am yours forever', but it is Othello who is bound to Iago, 'ensnared' for the time being 'body and soul'. We recall 'Perdition catch my soul'; and indeed 'chaos' seems 'come again'.

It is often maintained that from this time onwards Othello is cold, controlled in his determination to carry out the necessary act of justice; but it is not so simple as that, for love is not gone with the saying. The terrible inner conflict goes on. Iago's manipulation becomes even more skilled and relentless, and the handkerchief, as the only 'proof', plays its special part.

The next scene is Othello's attempt to 'prove' what is the truth by questioning Desdemona about the handkerchief. Here it becomes evident why this small object has more even than its double sentimental value. In two long passages of superb poetry the Othello music breaks into the harshness of the scene, resembling closely the tone of his account of his courtship, invested with some of the same serious wonder, but with a stronger and more ominous note of superstition. One almost feels that Othello believes in the 'magic in the web of it' as he recounts the tale of the 'charmer' who 'could almost read the thoughts of people', and gave the enchanted handkerchief to Othello's mother. These predominantly monosyllabic words add to the childlike solemnity:

> . . . she dying gave it me,
> And bid me when my fate would have me wive,
> To give it her; I did so, and take heed on't,
> Make it a darling, like your precious eye,
> To lose, or give't away, were such perdition
> As nothing else could match. (III, iv, 61–6)

To Desdemona's wondering, frightened 'Is't possible?', Othello answers with words full of all the strangeness of his earlier tales of adventure, attributing the powers of the handkerchief to its strange origin. Perhaps Iago's 'proof' would have convinced Othello if it had been just any handkerchief; there is a great deal of luck on his side, and there is Othello's rash and unreflecting nature—and Desdemona's lie. Once again, however, it is the language which makes the point. At this dramatic moment Shakespeare does not slip in two long passages of incantatory verse simply as decoration; later scenes confirm, too, the value Othello attaches to this handkerchief. Here, he speaks 'startingly and rash' in the agony of his suspicion; Desdemona's frightened lie seems to confirm his fears; then, still more hapless, she tries to turn him from the subject by pleading for Cassio, her entreaties punctuated by frenzied interjections from Othello, 'The handkerchief'.

After Cassio has found the handkerchief and given it to Bianca, Iago again refers to it; his mode of reassuring Othello is exactly that which must inflame him further. Even if Cassio does have it, it is really of no significance, especially as there is something more important: Cassio has 'blabbed', though 'no more than he'll unswear'. Pressed, Iago again feigns reluctance to say more, then finally says, hesitantly, 'Lie . . . With her, on her, what you will'. In the tortured jumble of Othello's next speech he mentions the handkerchief three times, then falls to the ground.

And still Iago does not let up. As Othello regains consciousness his torturer's tactics change yet again. Now he simply wishes Othello would bear his fortune 'like a man'. Millions of others are cuckolds; it is not too serious. Not surprisingly, this does not pacify Othello. Shortly he is given a form of 'ocular proof' when he actually sees 'my handkerchief' in the hands of Cassio's whore.

After this, and for the rest of the scene, it is touching and painful to see the pull of Othello's love, his struggle against belief in Desdemona's disloyalty. First, his desire for vengeance centres on Cassio: 'How shall I murder him, Iago?'; then, despite Iago's needling reference to Desdemona, he goes on 'I would have him nine years a-killing'. In what follows, Iago reaches the peak of his relentless cruelty, for *five times* Othello refers to Desdemona in an agony of love and regret for what he imagines to be the corruption of love—no less than five times, each more piteous than the last, culminating in:

> . . . but yet the pity of it Iago:
> O, Iago, the pity of it, Iago! (IV, i, 191–2)

This last anguished cry, infinitely pitiful, addressed three times *by name* to Iago, making it a direct appeal to another human being and friend, meets the total pitilessness of the torturer, who once again shifts his tactics, with more advice: of course, if Othello does not object to her 'iniquity' he should let her go on as she is, for it does not concern anyone else. The implication is strong that the iniquity is a fact and will go on. This Othello cannot endure: 'I will chop her into messes', and Iago presses his point home: Desdemona is 'foul', 'fouler'. Leavis claims Othello's love to be a 'characteristic voluptuousness', 'voluptuous sensuality'.[14] As noted, the sensual element is present in Othello's love, but in lines from

14 *The Common Pursuit*, pp. 149, 150.

this scene to which Leavis does not refer, Othello speaks of his wife with loving regret as a person, not merely as a tempting body: 'so delicate with her needle', 'an admirable musician', 'of so high and plenteous wit and invention', and so on. It denatures and falsifies the tragedy to devalue Othello's love to mere lust.

In the brutal brothel scene Desdemona feels 'fury in your words' as Othello accuses her of being false. Her anguished and touching 'to whom, my lord, with whom? how am I false?' prompts him to groan 'O, Desdemona, away, away, away', and weep. Mere lust might turn to hatred; Othello's love can never do so. The imagery of the beautiful lines already quoted (*cf.* pp. 38–9) shows that it is indeed the corruption of his love that Othello mistakenly mourns, and the rest of the speech expresses the mingled elements of love, sexual jealousy, and moral horror which make up Othello's torment.

At the beginning of the murder scene, Othello tries to be cold and controlled, but in the course of it the handkerchief comes in in such a way as to stir him to final passionate rage. He tries to see the murder as essential 'sacrifice' but the sight of his wife in innocent sleep does 'unprovide' his mind, and he must kiss her and weep again, and convince himself that justice requires him to strike where he loves. As he gnaws his lip, rolls his eyes, Desdemona, awake and seeing that 'some bloody passion' is shaking him, asks what is the matter. Significantly, for it seems to show that it is of the handkerchief as his only 'proof' that he is thinking in order to keep himself nerved to his purpose, he replies at once: 'That handkerchief which I so loved and gave thee/Thou gav'st to Cassio'. Although she denies it, Othello returns twice 'I saw my handkerchief in's hand'; 'I saw the handkerchief'. As Desdemona protests her innocence and asks for Cassio to be sent for, she learns of his death, and, still hapless ('Desdemona' means 'unfortunate'), grieves for him. It is this which enrages Othello and, renewedly convinced of her guilt, he kills her in the end not as a cold act of justice but in a moment of angry passion.

The handkerchief is important right up to the closing scenes of the play. Torn with grief after the murder, Othello seeks final justification, to others and to himself, for what he has done, as he says 'O, she was foul', and adduces as final proof Desdemona's gift to Cassio:

> . . . I saw it in his hand:
> It was a handkerchief, an antique token
> My father gave my mother. (V, ii, 216–18)

Again the simple beauty of the poetry expresses perfectly Othello's feelings of grief and betrayal. Soon after this, Emilia reveals the truth, and when Othello next speaks it is to turn to Iago with 'Are there no stones in heaven/But what serve for the thunder?' The final reference to the handkerchief (it is still on Othello's mind) is in the last quiet question 'How came you, Cassio, by a handkerchief that was my wife's?' (V, ii, 320-1). When Cassio's reply confirms what Othello has just learned, giving the final proof that his just sacrifice is a terrible murder, he can only groan 'O, fool, fool, fool', and after the superb final speech carry out his last act of justice.

The Othello Music: Harmony and Discord

To note some striking and consistent contrasts in the speech patterns of the two principal characters will throw light on all the previous discussion and lead on to a final comment on the play's last scene.

Seeing or even reading *Othello* for the first time, one might be left with the impression that Othello speaks in poetry, Iago in prose, with perhaps a further impression that Othello's speech is the more elaborate and contains more long words. Both impressions oversimplify, for Iago sometimes speaks in poetry, Othello in prose, and both use at times long and uncommon words. It is the pace and thrust of Iago's poetry or prose which places it at the opposite pole from Othello's:

> . . . You shall mark
> Many a duteous and knee-crooking knave,
> That, doting on his own obsequious bondage,
> Wears out his time much like his master's ass,
> For nought but provender, and when he's old, cashiered,
> Whip me such honest knaves: others there are,
> Who, trimm'd in forms, and visages of duty,
> Keep yet their hearts attending on themselves,
> And throwing but shows of service on their lords,
> Do well thrive by 'em, and when they have lin'd their coats,
> Do themselves homage, those fellows have some soul,
> And such a one do I profess myself . . . (I, i, 44-55)

Poetic images and long words do nothing here to slow the quick movement, to which the light punctuation contributes (there is only one colon). Although Iago habitually speaks with some emphasis, almost all his speeches call for quick light stressing rather than anything more ponderous. His 'put money in thy purse' speech (I, iii, 335–62) is a good example, as are all his speeches to Roderigo. In Iago's compulsive hatred of the good and beautiful, there is an attacking energetic quality which issues in this manner of speaking.

His speech-rhythms become uncharacteristically slower and smoother only when he is dissimulating. This occurs in his 'Can he be angry?' speech, because of the concern which he is carefully feigning. During the temptation of Othello, most of Iago's speeches are markedly less staccato, less directly attacking, than usual, because he is playing a part, pretending always to speak hesitatingly and reluctantly. He is made to adapt his speech very closely to the circumstances: after the sacrilege of Othello's 'Now, by yond marble heaven' oath, Iago too kneels and

>   . . . doth give up
> The excellency (execution, F) of his will, hand, heart,
> To wrong'd Othello's service (III, iii, 472–4)

and his whole speech, flowing straight on from Othello's, is a direct parody of Othello's characteristic music.

Othello's speech is, above all, flowing. Its ordered harmonies are expressive of the ordered universe in which he lives (with good and evil at opposite poles and clearly distinguishable) until Iago throws him into a state of confusion ('chaos') and moral horror by convincing him that Desdemona is guilty and that therefore good and evil are horribly intertwined. The ordered harmonies of his normal speech, the 'Othello music', are broken or speeded up when he is thus influenced by Iago's poison. Indeed, it has often been noted that it is really Iago we are hearing in Othello's speech when the music is wholly untuned: 'I'll chop her into messes'; 'Goats and monkeys!' (and in many other instances of ugly animal-imagery); 'Hot, hot, and moist, this hand . . .' with all the rest of this speech (III, iv, 35–40); the chaos of 'Lie with her, lie on her? . . . Handkerchief?—O, devil!' (IV, i, 35–43).

Although Iago at times brings chaos into Othello's speech, the Othello music in many moods runs right through the play. When we first see Othello, the whole scene contrasts his nature and manner with Iago's— very strikingly within these few lines alone:

Iago: There are the raised father and his friends,
    You were best go in.

Othello: Not I; I must be found.
            My parts, my title, and my perfect soul
            Shall manifest me rightly: . . . (I, ii, 29–32)

In the first line, Iago is continuing his efforts to rouse Othello to fear and flight or to resentment and action: inside a single line, the urgency of his incisive 'You were best go in' modulates to Othello's measured 'Not I; I must be found', the repetition and the punctuation enforcing the slower pace which is sustained in the rest of the speech. The slow stresses of:

        Most potent, grave, and reverend signiors,
        My very noble and approved good masters,
        That I have ta'en away this old man's daughter,
        It is most true; true I have married her . . . (I, iii, 76–9)

are very expressive of Othello's dignity, respect for the signiory, and his grave forthrightness. The repetition which plays a part here in slowing down the verse and adding emphasis is characteristic of Othello's speech, other examples (among many) occurring at I, iii, 91–2; IV, ii, 57; V, ii, 1–3; V, ii, 345–9.

When we first see Othello assert authority, the music is not yet untuned. The verse rolls majestically, not only in longer words but in the flow of heavy monosyllables:

        For Christian shame, put by this barbarous brawl;
        He that stirs next to carve for his own rage
        Holds his soul light, he dies upon his motion;
        Silence that dreadful bell, it frights the isle
        From her propriety . . . (II, iii, 163–7)

There is great force here, but it is only as he becomes angry in the 'Now by heaven' speech that we hear the premonitory rumbling of the storm, of which the relentless and terrible power is expressed fully in the Pontic sea speech (III, iii, 460–7), where the 'music' is magnificent, but the whole speech is a terrible parody. This is a matter of form and content: superficially the Othello-poetry is at its most splendid, but there sounds through its flow the pure Iago-discord which has caught Othello's soul and broken the harmony of his universe (cf. p. 15).

If the Othello-poetry seems most haunting when Othello is suffering most, and if beauty and longing become then most jumbled with ugliness (as in the brothel scene), this is because to Othello the universe as Iago makes him see it is contradictory and incomprehensible; nothing can resolve the resulting conflict in his soul. Different aspects of Othello's love and agony find expression in varied music. The soaring happiness of 'O, my soul's joy' is darkened by the 'If's', by the wonder at his good fortune which leads to 'fear' that

> My soul hath her content so absolute
> That not another comfort like to this
> Succeeds in unknown fate. (II, i, 191–3) (*cf.* p. 42)

with later the anguish of 'But there where I have garner'd up my heart'; the regretful grief of 'Nay had she been true . . .'; the poignant conviction that ' 'Tis pitiful; but yet Iago knows that she with Cassio hath the act of shame a thousand times committed'.

Monosyllables compose some of the play's finest lines: they, too, show the contrast in pace (and thus in characterisation) already noted. Iago's 'Though I do hate him as I hate hell-pains', 'I must show out a flag and sign of love', 'It makes us or it mars us, think of that', all demand a quick and urgent delivery. Othello's:

> 'Tis well I am found by you.
> I will but spend a word here in the house
> And go with you. (I, ii, 47–9)

and his 'Keep up your bright swords for the dew will rust 'em' demand the opposite, as does the elegiac woe of 'My wife, my wife, my wife; I ha' no wife' and 'Now; how dost thou look now? O ill-starr'd wench,/ Pale as thy smock, . . . cold, cold, my girl . . .' (*cf.* p. 66).

This brings us to the play's last scene. Here is T. S. Eliot's dictum:

> What Othello seems to me to be doing in making this speech is *cheering himself up*. He is endeavouring to escape reality, he has ceased to think about Desdemona and is thinking about himself. Humility is the most difficult of all virtues to achieve; nothing dies harder than the desire to think well of oneself. Othello succeeds in turning himself into a pathetic figure by adopting an *aesthetic* rather than a moral attitude dramatising himself against his environment.[15] (The italics are Eliot's.)

Dr. Leavis's pronouncement echoes Eliot's: 'unmistakably self-dramatisation'.[16] I quote these views only to urge their rejection, for

---

[15] "Shakespeare and the Stoicism of Seneca", a lecture to the Shakespeare Association, London, 1927, now most readily available in Eliot's *Selected Essays*, 1951.

[16] *The Common Pursuit*, p. 152.

they have long exercised a disproportionate and pernicious influence on *Othello*-criticism. There is much support for their rejection. Among many others, Dover Wilson argues cogently against them in his Introduction to the Cambridge *Othello*. Particularly impressive is John Holloway's brilliant Appendix to a fine book; he not only disagrees with Leavis's argument, but analyses it rigorously and points out its serious flaws.

In this scene, what we are seeing is an Othello who has come to know that his moral world *is*, after all, as he has believed it to be; good and evil are once again at opposite poles, now that he knows Iago is hellishly evil, Desdemona of heavenly goodness. There is no more confusion in Othello's mind: he has murdered what he best loves and for him there can now be only 'perdition'. He will carry out the necessary act of justice believing that he is not only sending himself to the certain torments of the damned, but that this includes eternal separation from Desdemona. In his final speech there is the emotion of a measureless and hopeless grief, but no emotional or moral confusion, no emotional centring on self. Order and calm have returned with certainty of the justice of what must now be done. He dismisses his past services: 'No more of that'. His great love and terrible perplexity are to be recorded, but nothing must be extenuated. Having thrown away the pearl of great price, he can only weep without restraint, but these are not the sort of tears to be accompanied by sobs, heaves of the body, or facial contortions. Othello is quite still, his face composed almost to a mask of grief; the tears fall as of their own volition, heavily, and with a natural force suggested by the dropping of gum from the Arabian trees. It is not likely that an actor will be able to produce this flow of tears, but Shakespeare gives him the three slow, flowing lines of the simile with which to create the illusion. After comparing his actions to those of a violent and treacherous heathen, he strikes the blow of justice with all the confidence and control of the old Othello (compare this with Antony's bungling attempt).

All through the play, the words have shown the very opposite of a self-centred, self-dramatising Othello: here any note of this would be out of keeping with his grief and with the mood of the final couplet. This poignantly recalls the harmony, the 'too much of joy', when the couple kissed after being reunited; now there is only the poor harmony of a kiss before death:

> I kiss'd thee when I kill'd thee, no way but this,
> Killing myself, to die upon a kiss.

Othello and Revenge: A Verdict?

Insofar as they were believing Christians, Elizabethans would consider revenge wrong; insofar as they were Renaissance pagans, they would *feel* it to be right. From this conflict springs much of the tension which is felt in revenge tragedy.

Although, as noted, the usual charges against Othello cannot stand, there is one thing for which he must be condemned: his assumption that revenge is appropriate to justice and that killing is appropriate to revenge. This assumption lies so deep as never even to be questioned; without coming directly into the tragic action, it thus overshadows it and makes tragedy—this particular tragedy—inevitable. Othello's doubts are bound up only with Desdemona's guilt, not with the question of what to do if she be guilty. The 'black vengeance' invoked is more monstrous and blameworthy than mere jealousy, which need not have led to murder or to any terrible revenge. His 'bloody thoughts' which make him wish 'the slave had forty lives! One is too poor, too weak for my revenge' is 'foul disproportion' so black and terrible as to make *Othello* (although it is not a revenge play) Shakespeare's most profound and haunting presentation of revenge.

It is *Hamlet* which forces us to *think* most about revenge, raising the timeless question, among others: is there any appropriate way of dealing with accomplished evil? It is *Othello* which makes us *feel* most about revenge. Francis Bacon in his essay 'Of Revenge' says: 'Revenge is a kind of wild justice.' Othello's revenge is that—a black wrong the more terrible for being committed by a man 'more fair than black'. The facts of his tragic misapprehension and of Desdemona's heavenly goodness make it worse because the black deed becomes also a terrible and *irreversible mistake*—with the timeless questions which this raises.

The real enemy within Othello is the lust for revenge which grows in response to Iago's poison (it is Othello himself who first thinks in terms of killing: 'I will tear her all to pieces', III, iii, 438). With any other response, all of Iago's horrible mischief would have failed to bring about the tragedy.

Appendices

A. Double Time in 'Othello'

It is plain that there is not one time-sequence in *Othello*, but two. Once the characters are in Cyprus, all the events take place within about thirty-six hours, and we are made aware of the passage of time by references to night, morning, meal-times, evening, night again. Yet the lapse of a longer (even a much longer) period is strongly implied. The most obvious need for the short-time scheme, besides the dramatic intensity it provides, is that Iago's plot can succeed only if no one (and particularly Othello) has the chance to find him out. The most obvious need for the long-time scheme is that if adultery is alleged to have occurred (whether 'a thousand times' or just a few) there must have been some opportunity for it.

There are too many excellent discussions of this subject for me to wish to cover the ground yet again in detail. Granville Barker, Bradley, and many others have gone into it very thoroughly. M. R. Ridley discusses it usefully in the Arden *Othello*, and Dover Wilson's discussion in the Cambridge *Othello* lists precise references to passages where long-time is implied. In the Furness *Variorum* can be found much of North's original discussion of it in 1850.

It is perhaps worth noting that some critics have worried a good deal about whether Shakespeare knew what he was doing or simply made a bad mistake (which is not noticed too much until one starts to study it). Recently Ned B. Allen has produced an explanation,[1] maintaining in ingenious detail that Shakespeare first wrote part of the play, probably the last three acts, returning to write the rest after a lapse of time. Allen does not believe Shakespeare planned the two time-schemes but, noticing them when putting the play together, did not consider it necessary to eliminate the discrepancies. This theory does account for what we find in the play, and Allen argues it well and persuasively, but of course it is most unlikely ever to be proved.

Interesting as the theory is, it is in a sense irrelevant: or, rather, what matters more is to look at the play primarily from the standpoint of the

[1] 'The Two Parts of *Othello*', *Shakespeare Survey*, 21, pp. 13–29.

audiences for whom Shakespeare wrote his plays. Once again a comment from Dr. Bradbrook makes the relevant point aptly:

> The Elizabethans were not trained to put two and two together in the matter of temporal sequence, and so these difficulties did not exist for them. . . . [The heightened suspense, attention, and excitement justify] the logical contradiction, and the well-knit appearance of a play like *Othello* is its own justification.[2]

This means (as Allen suggests, too) that Shakespeare would simply not need to worry about time discrepancies so long as they served his dramatic purposes.

B. *Alterations to Cinthio's Tale*

1. The creation of Roderigo serves two ends which are closely related. Iago, in revealing much of his true nature to him, reveals it to the audience, and we, outside the play, enjoy (or suffer) a terrible irony: we are always aware that no one but Roderigo within the play is given any such revelation. As we watch Roderigo go on trusting Iago when he has good reason for mistrust, we are the more painfully aware that Othello is ignorant of what Iago is, and is correspondingly defenceless against his Machiavellian practice.

2. In Iago the obvious and straightforward motivation of the wicked ensign is removed.

3. The account of Othello's courtship is added.

4. The brawl scene is expanded from a single sentence.

5. The storm occurs.

6. An element of magic and wonder is associated with the fatal handkerchief.

7. Othello's marriage is of much shorter duration than the Moor's. Similarly, in Cinthio, the tragic (or melodramatic) action covers a much longer period.

8. In the original version, the ensign's wife knows of her husband's schemes and is too afraid of him to reveal them; when she finally defies him, it is only in refusing to co-operate in the actual murder of Disdemona. Shakespeare's conception of the character, within the dramatic whole, demands Emilia's unbelieving reiteration of 'my husband'. The audience must feel the shock to her of this revelation and thrill to her quick and courageous defiance of Iago. If, however, we are tempted to share too much her anger as she reveals to Othello his tragic error, to see

[2] *Themes and Conventions of Elizabethan Tragedy*, p. 14.

him as she does, and as he sees himself ('O, fool, fool, fool'), Shakespeare has provided this corrective: even Iago's wife has not known him for what he is.

9. The element of Machiavellian practice is made much stronger in *Othello*. Cinthio's Moor is much more easily tricked, and in the end he and the ensign plot together to kill Disdemona. They carry out the murder in such a way as to make it look accidental, first clubbing her over the head with a stocking filled with sand and then bringing down the roof on her bed. Shakespeare has transformed this, the crudest possible melodrama, into the pathos and tragedy of Act V.

10. In Cinthio, the story goes dragging on after the murder. The Moor does not kill himself, but escapes justice, and it is only long afterwards that Disdemona's family find him and avenge her death by killing him. The ensign's story drags on, too: he eventually succumbs to internal injuries resulting from prolonged torture.

11. Because of the Turkish threat Othello is given responsibility for the defence of Cyprus. This has seldom been taken to have much significance to the tragedy; what significance Shakespeare intended is not certain, but Emrys Jones has recently written a useful article which should encourage more study of the question. A brief extract shows one possible approach:

> Shakespeare could, of course, have taken for granted a general interest in the Ottoman empire which is very remote from what a modern audience brings to *Othello*. The Turkish menace to Christendom was a fact in Shakespeare's entire lifetime; it remained of pressing concern to the West until late in the seventeenth century. This fact may, of itself, have given *Othello's* Cypriot setting an ominous character which is lost on us. As Knolles puts it: 'The Venetians had ever had great care of the island of Cyprus, as lying far from them, in the midst of the sworn enemies of the Christian religion, and had therefore often times determined to have fortified the same.' So Cyprus could be seen as an outpost of Christendom, rich, vulnerable, and perilously situated: a highly suitable setting for a play showing Christian behaviour under stress. After Cassio's drunken brawl has been put down, Othello is to say: 'Are we turn'd Turk, and to ourselves do that /Which heaven hath forbid the Ottomites?/ For Christian shame, put by this barbarous brawl.' His words, skilfully placed in the scene, are emphatic and ironic. For if Shakespeare's fictitious action can be said to belong to the years 1570–71, those were historically the very years when Cyprus underwent a violent conversion from Christian to Turkish rule—the years when it literally 'turn'd Turk'.[3]

[3] 'Othello, Lepanto, and the Cyprus Wars', *Shakespeare Survey*, 21, pp. 47–52.

Yet again we see the necessity of considering Shakespeare's plays in their Elizabethan context. And yet another nuance is added to the Othello-Iago antithesis: Othello himself temporarily 'turns Turk' under Iago's barbarous influence.

C. 'Othello' and 'The Winter's Tale'

Some contrasts between these plays are relevant to understanding *Othello*.

Too often Othello and Leontes are bracketed as similar, almost identical, instances of the 'easily jealous' man—a serious misconception. In *Othello*, Shakespeare shows a man painfully and skilfully 'wrought' to jealousy; in Leontes, a man whose jealousy is a 'diseas'd opinion' entirely self-engendered and self-perpetuated. Many of the details of the circumstances in which Leontes becomes jealous, and remains so, are almost exactly opposite to those in which we see Othello.

Leontes, as king in his own land, suffers from none of the social or racial factors which complicate Othello's case: Othello is both racially and socially an outsider; not knowing the Venetian society into which he marries he cannot enjoy the security which Leontes has. Unlike Othello, Leontes is long married and can be supposed to know his wife well. Then too he is surrounded by people who assure him Hermione is innocent, swear to it in the strongest terms, and keep pleading with him to believe in her. Among these are the wholly 'worthy' and trustworthy Paulina, and the loyal and honourable Camillo, to whom the king's distrust spreads immediately, and for no reason. Othello has only Emilia to counteract the influence of Iago, whom, with much reason, he trusts and whose word he therefore takes in preference to that of a 'simple bawd'.

Like Othello, Leontes becomes prey to his jealousy, a hunted creature, but he is prey to his own false view, not to a skilful torturer. The difference can become very clear in stage presentations of the two plays. It is convincing and right for Leontes's self-generated suspicions to keep him in agonised and ceaseless movement, while many people in many ways try to reason with him and calm him. Othello, quite alone with Iago in his temptation, is relentlessly harried by Iago's varied attacks. Audiences should find both men pitiable, but Othello should seem much the more pitiable. He is like a great helpless beast as his tormentor prods and whips him verbally to a restless frenzied movement which reflects his mental confusion and utter misery.

Interestingly, the changes which Shakespeare made in his two sources markedly strengthen these contrasts (*cf.* Appendix B), Leontes becomes jealous much more suddenly than Pandosto, whose 'doubtful thoughts' are shown to develop to 'secret mistrust', and only gradually to 'flaming jealousy'. Leontes's grounds for suspicion are made much slighter. In *The Winter's Tale* great weight is given to the universal support which Hermione receives from the court; there is no one who does not believe in her. Pandosto's nobles try only to persuade him not to burn his wife and baby 'without due proof', and plead for mercy for the queen 'even if she had faulted'. Camillo is made an unquestionably honourable counsellor, whereas the corresponding figure in Greene is much less so. After the young prince's death, Pandosto's queen falls down dead, and Pandosto is prevented by courtiers from killing himself. Most important of all, there is in the original none of the penitence and reconciliation of *The Winter's Tale*. Pandosto feels guilt and remorse for the death of his wife, son, and baby daughter (for he believes her dead), and he mourns for them, but at the end of sixteen years, there is none of the continuing 'saint-like sorrow' of Leontes. Pandosto's daughter and her lover are brought to the king's court and Pandosto (without knowing who she is) falls in love with her, tries hard to win her from her lover, and threatens her when she refuses to become his concubine. After finding out that she is his daughter, he sinks into a state of melancholy guilt and finally kills himself.

It may be argued that I give too much weight to these changes, for after all, in creating poetic drama from rambling prose narratives, Shakespeare was bound to tighten up and alter his material. The fact remains that his changes *in both sources* are wholly consistent with the totally different reactions which audiences must feel at the close of stage presentations of *Othello* and *The Winter's Tale*. The view of life which seems to lie behind *Othello* is radically different from that behind *The Winter's Tale*. In the later play Shakespeare begins by showing tragic disruption worse than anything in *Othello*. The audience sees Leontes break successively every sort of natural bond: with his brother-king, with his trusted courtiers, with his wife. The young prince, because of his father's behaviour, dies from grief, thus breaking the line of succession to the throne. Leontes denies that his daughter is his own, and orders her to be cast out to what he means to be death. He utters savage threats to burn to death or otherwise kill his wife and all those whom he mistrusts. He is as much 'tyrant' as he is 'jealous', continuing to assert his own flawed judgement against all others until his final cry 'There is no truth at all in the oracle'. The audience watches disruption within his own mind bring disruption and death into his family and into the order of the state, and should feel a shock of horror as he finally challenges the cosmic order by his defiance of Apollo's oracle.

But in *The Winter's Tale*, divine powers preside, permitting the re-establishment of some degree of harmony at the end. There is a wonderful dramatic link (achieved through poetry) between the Leontes who is being led away to 'these sorrows' at the end of Act III and the Leontes of the beginning of Act V, whom we may actually see on his knees, but who will in any case be seen to be still grieving and penitent. It is after this long period of grief and repentance that we see him receive back his queen and his daughter; and this seems to have come about through the operation of something very like a religious sense of 'grace'—ideas of grace and sanctity being associated throughout with Hermione. In *Othello*, we do not see the operation of any such grace. As in Hardy (*Tess of the D'Urbervilles*), no providence intervenes to prevent tragedy. The heavens, despite appeals to them, seem as empty as they do in Camus (*Le Malentendu*) or Sartre (*Le Diable et Le Bon Dieu*).

D. Othello and Some Other Shakespearian Lovers

It is a commonplace to say that in presenting human emotions and behaviour, Shakespeare is an absolute master. This is true of his lovers, of whom we see and hear in his plays an astonishing variety. Since others have seen Othello's love as self-centred lust, and since I have argued strongly that there is an identifiable quality in his love which is of great beauty, and that this is conveyed through language, it is relevant to look at the different sorts of language associated with some other Shakespearian lovers. In each case, bearing in mind the role of the particular lover within his particular play, we see that the tone, the precise quality, of the lover and of his love are shown with marvellous rightness.

Sometimes we are shown 'love' which is not love at all, as in the mannered, in-love-with-love effusions of Orsino (on Olivia) or Romeo (on Rosaline). In *Much Ado About Nothing*, Claudio's praises of Hero express sentiments not much deeper:

> In mine eyes she is the sweetest lady that I
> ever looked on. (I, ii)

Into his mind, now conveniently 'vacant' of 'war-thoughts',

> Come thronging soft and delicate desires
> All prompting me how fair young Hero is. (I, ii)

The words, whether prose, or verse, are pleasant, but reflect the thinness of Claudio's love. Callow and inexperienced, he readily believes the worst of his lady and refers to her as 'this rotten orange', having deliberately waited to shame her until the wedding ceremony itself. Within the same play, we feel Benedick's love to be deeper and more interesting. Watching and enjoying the early battles of wit between Benedick and Beatrice, we soon feel the genuine attraction of kindred merry natures. Both are more than merry: as Beatrice grieves after Hero's humiliation, we should be moved when a very serious Benedick says:

> I do love nothing in the world so well as you.
> Is not that strange? (IV, i)

Shakespeare shows, too, varied and convincing instances of love as lust. In *Measure for Measure*, Angelo suddenly finds himself lusting 'foully' for Isabella. What he says expresses precisely his self-disgust and the ugliness which he recognises in his feelings for the pure girl:

> . . . it is I
> That, lying by the violet, in the sun
> Do, as the carrion does, not as the flower,
> Corrupt with virtuous season. (II, ii)

In a less blatant form, lust is dominant in *Troilus and Cressida*, a play about lechery and war, in which a young man idealises his passion for a slut and finds himself betrayed by her. Looking forward to meeting Cressida, Troilus's words convey sharp sexual excitement:

> I am giddy; expectation whirls me round,
> The imaginary relish is so sweet
> That it enchants my sense; what will it be
> When that the watery palate tastes indeed
> Love's thrice repured nectar? (III, ii)

When the lovers-to-be first meet soon after, they speak in a mannered and highly artificial prose, devoid of feeling. Parting from Cressida, Troilus speaks in a manner suggestive of sexual avidity. What he regrets is the interruption of a kind of love-making which, through the harsh sounds of the individual words and the jerky rhythm, is made to seem a physical striving without tenderness or satisfaction:

> And suddenly; where injury of chance
> Puts back leave-taking, justles roughly by
> All time of pause, rudely beguiles our lips
> Of all rejoindure, forcibly prevents
> Our lock'd embrasures, strangles our dear vows
> Even in the birth of our own lab'ring breath: . . .
> And scants us with a single famish'd kiss,
> Distasted with the salt of broken tears. (IV, iv)

Between this and Antony's 'dotage' we are made to feel a vast difference. Antony's emotions are much more complex. Certainly there is a strong element of lust, with emphasis on 'soft hours', 'my pleasure', and 'gawdy' nights of revelry. And there is ugliness in his passion; when angry and jealous he expresses savage contempt:

> I found you as a morsel cold upon
> Dead Caesar's trencher: (III, xiii)

Yet, in defeat and dishonour after following her 'fearful sails', we have seen him forget his anger and shame, and turn to comfort Cleopatra:

> Fall not a tear, I say; one of them rates
> All that is won and lost: give me a kiss;
> E'en this repays me. (III, xi)

Towards the end, when he believes that 'like a right gipsy' Cleopatra has betrayed him, he grieves, after an angry outburst, at the falsity of her, 'Whose heart I thought I had, for she had mine' (IV, xiv). All that he has done has been for her: by comparison kingdoms, fame, duty, even honour have seemed trivial. But if Antony's passion takes on a value so far beyond mere lust, it is not only because of the world-scale of the affair, but also because of the simple and loverlike delight he finds in the most ordinary activities when in her company. In the play's first scene, we see this wonderfully expressed in words which also convey something of Cleopatra's 'infinite variety' and enduring fascination:

> Fie, wrangling queen!
> Whom everything becomes, to chide, to laugh,
> To weep: how every passion fully strives
> To make itself, in thee, fair and admired!
> No messenger but thine, and all alone
> To-night we'll wander through the streets, and note
> The qualities of people.

This sets the tone: all Antony's later behaviour is consistent with what we see here, so that we are never surprised when Cleopatra '[nods] him back to her'.

Totally different is Romeo's youthful ardour for Juliet. There is nothing more touchingly and convincingly loverlike in all literature than:

> Juliet: I have forgot why I did call thee back.
> Romeo: Let me stand here till thou remember it.
> Juliet: I shall forget . . .
> Romeo: And I'll still stand to have thee still forget, (II, ii)

nor anything much lovelier than this, in the aubade:

> Let me be ta'en . . .
> I am content so thou wilt have it so.
> I'll say yon grey is not the morning's eye
> Nor that is not the lark . . .
> Come, death, and welcome! Juliet wills it so.
> How is't, my soul? let's talk, it is not day. (III, v)

nor anything more moving than the beautiful and terrible simplicity of:

> Well, Juliet, I will lie with thee tonight. (V, i)

Ferdinand, too, loves at first sight: his love's great worth is shown by his free and joyous acceptance of the heavy and menial tasks imposed as a test by Prospero. Being a prince, 'I do think, a king', he:

> . . . would no more endure
> This wooden slavery than to suffer
> The flesh-fly blow my mouth.—Hear my soul speak:-
> The very instant that I saw you, did
> My heart fly to your service; there resides
> To make me slave to it; and for your sake
> Am I this patient log-man.—(III, i)

In *The Winter's Tale* Shakespeare shows both youthful and mature love at their deepest. Florizel is sometimes, quite wrongly, regarded as no more than a conventional and colourless young lover, but the quality of his love is distinguished in several ways from anything so commonplace. His instincts are as strong as Troilus's, but he is in perfect control:

> . . . since my desires
> Run not before mine honour; nor my lust
> Burn hotter than my faith. (IV, iii)

He expresses his delight in his beloved:

> What you do
> Still betters what is done. When you speak, sweet,
> I'ld have you do it ever; when you sing,
> I'ld have you buy and sell so; so give alms,
> Pray so; for the ord'ring your affairs,
> To sing them, too: when you dance, I wish you
> A wave of the sea, that you might ever do
> Nothing but that; move still, still so. (IV, iii)

Without Perdita's love he can 'prize' neither high rank, his own youthful charm, nor great knowledge, and he rejects as impossible any 'violation of my faith':

> Not for Bohemia, nor the pomp that may
> Be thereat gleaned; for all the sun sees, or
> The close earth wombs, or the profound seas hide
> In unknown fathoms, will I break my oath
> To this, my fair beloved; (IV, iii)

The flexibility and perfection of the verse in this late play expresses a love youthful and ardent, yet mature in its control, and of proved devotion and constancy—richer than anything, however lovely, in the much earlier *Romeo and Juliet*.

In the middle-aged penitent Leontes, there is something deeper, and infinitely moving: love tested by sixteen years of suffering. Appreciation of the worth of the beloved has been heightened by loss and by continuing remorse for 'she I killed' and for the virtues of the 'sweet'st companion that e'er man/ Bred his hopes out of'. There is warm sensuality, but assimilated in a love which feels equally its spiritual loss. Leontes realises:

> I might have looked upon my queen's full eyes,
> Have taken treasure from her lips. (V, i)

Remembering all he has lost, he must remain faithful to her memory:

> . . . Stars, stars
> And all eyes else dead coals. Fear thou no wife,
> I'll have no wife, Paulina. (V, i)

Later, Leontes's immobility before the statue, and his anguished refusal to allow the curtain to be drawn, should so communicate to the audience the depth of his emotion that they share his incredulous joy when the cold stone turns out to be living flesh and he breathes 'O, she's warm . . .' a line as beautiful in its simplicity as any in Shakespeare (*cf.* p. 54 for poignant contrasts with Othello).

Before returning finally to Othello's love, it is interesting to see the frightful contrast to it which Shakespeare presents in Iago's attitude to love. His lusts are shown to be exceptionally ugly, uglier than the examples cited above. Angelo at least recognises the ugliness of his sudden desire. There is something genuine in Troilus's passion. Iago feels nothing for anyone. In talking of 'our raging motions, our carnal stings, our unbitted lusts, whereof I take this, that you call love to be a sect or scion' (I, iii, 330–33), he shows that he sees no meaning in love. To him it must be a mere incomprehensible offshoot of lust. Through the generalising 'our', he attributes his own feelings to all. Traversi has pointed out that there is something very revealing in the phrases Iago uses: they certainly suggest a particularly driving and tormenting sort of lust—a quality which the harsh staccato prose should enforce upon the actor of the part. Iago's confident prediction about the 'changeable' Moor is another generalisation from his own experience:

> The food that to him now is as luscious as locusts,
> Shall be to him shortly as acerb as the coloquintida. (I, iii, 349–50)

Desdemona too 'must have change, she must', he insists, once she is 'sated with his body'. This tells us nothing about Othello or Desdemona, but everything about Iago, and we can now perhaps make more sense of the contradiction when he predicts (in soliloquy) that Othello will be a good husband to Desdemona (cf. p. 32). The explanation may be that Iago himself knows only a cold yet burning lust which must always, and soon, end in satiety and disgust. He can see that there is for others something finer in love than this, but since his nature prevents him from understanding or experiencing it, he wants only to destroy it.

No figure could present a greater contrast to Iago than Othello, radiant with joy in his spiritual and sensual union, marvelling at shared happiness. His generous nature gives him an almost boundless capacity for the love Iago cannot understand. This gives point to G. F. Hibbard's comment that Othello is about 'the wanton destruction of happiness'.[4]

In each of the plays referred to above, Shakespeare's language is matched to the quality of the emotion he is showing and to the role of each lover within a dramatic and poetic whole. We may think of these or of any other Shakespearian lovers, but only in The Winter's Tale does the beauty of the language equal that of the words in which expression is given to Othello's love—and to Desdemona's love, for they are not separable. Othello's joy in his love is a reflection of Desdemona's own radiance. There is her '. . . but here's my husband' as he waits at the Sagittary to hear what she will have to say (I, iii, 185); her 'My dear Othello' as they are reunited in Cyprus. These moments can, on the stage, be almost intolerably moving; the words are simple but lend themselves to acting which makes very clear the beauty of their love—with Desdemona's loving gentleness and warmth calling forth Othello's warmest and most joyous response. The more the audience is made aware of the spiritual quality of the union (later, too, of its sensual quality, which, again, can be suggested very well on the stage) and of Iago's twisted, self-imprisoned sexuality, the more painful it will be to watch the progress of a tragedy which, as Hibbard suggests, shows above all the relentless attack of hatred and envy upon a shared love (cf. p. 40).

[4] 'Othello and Shakespearian Tragedy', Shakespeare Survey, 21, p. 43.

Bibliography

Chapter 1

H. Kögeritz and C. T. Prouty, Photo-Facsimile Edition (1 vol.) of Shakespeare's *Comedies, Histories, and Tragedies* (*the First Folio of 1623*), London, 1955

C. Praetorius, Introduction H. A. Evans, A Facsimile of *Othello* (the First Quarto, 1622), London, 1885

C. Praetorius, Introduction H. A. Evans, A Facsimile of *Othello* (the Second Quarto, 1630), London, 1885

H. H. Furness, *Variorum* Edition of Shakespeare's Plays (Vol. VI, *Othello*), Philadelphia, 1886. My page references are to this edition, but also apply to a paperback edition now available (Dover Publications). Furness's edition cannot be too highly recommended to students at all levels for its illuminating comments by critics and noted actors.

Shakespeare, *Othello*, ed. H. C. Hart (Arden), London, 1903

Shakespeare, *Othello*, ed. M. R. Ridley (New Arden), London, 1958

Shakespeare, *Othello*, ed. Alice Walker and John Dover Wilson (New Cambridge), 1957

Shakespeare, *Othello*, ed. F. C. Holroyd and R. E. C. Houghton (New Clarendon), Oxford, 1968

E. A. J. Honigmann, *The Stability of Shakespeare's Texts*, London, 1965. (The chapter on *Othello* is useful.)

Fredson Bowers, *Editing*, University of Pennsylvania, 1955

W. W. Greg, *The Editorial Problem in Shakespeare*, Oxford, 1954

W. W. Greg, *The Shakespeare First Folio*, Oxford, 1955

Alice Walker, *Textual Problems of the First Folio*, Cambridge, 1953

Charlton Hinman, *Printing and Proof-Reading of the First Folio* (2 vols.), Oxford, 1963

Chapter 2

M. C. Bradbrook, *Themes and Conventions of Elizabethan Tragedy*, Cambridge, 1935

M. C. Bradbrook, *Elizabethan Stage Conditions*, Hamden, Conn., 1932. (A paperback edition is now available.)

L. C. Knights, 'How Many Children Had Lady Macbeth?', *Explorations*, London, 1946

Louis B. Wright, *Middle Class Culture in Elizabethan England*, Chapel Hill, North Carolina, 1935

Sister Miriam Joseph, 'Rhetoric', in *A Shakespeare Encyclopedia*, ed. Campbell and Quinn, London, 1966

I. A. Richards, *The Philosophy of Rhetoric*, New York, 1936 (pp. 127 ff.)

E. K. Chambers, *The Elizabethan Stage*, Oxford, 1923

J. C. Adams, *The Globe Playhouse*, Cambridge, Mass., 1942; London, 1961

Studies in Shakespeare, ed. Peter Alexander, London, 1964, contains two essays relevant to this chapter: Richard David, 'Shakespeare and the Players'; H. S. Bennett, 'Shakespeare's Audience'.

A. C. Bradley's *Oxford Lectures on Poetry*, London, 1965, contains an essay on 'Shakespeare's Theatre and Audience'.

Hilda M. Hulme, *Explorations in Shakespeare's Language*, London, 1962

Chapter 3

Theodore Spencer, *Shakespeare and the Nature of Man*, Cambridge, 1943

Caroline Spurgeon, *Shakespeare's Imagery*, Cambridge, 1965

R. B. Heilman, 'More Fair Than Black: Light and Dark in *Othello*', *Essays in Criticism*, October 1951

Winthrop Jordan, *White Over Black*, Chapel Hill, North Carolina, 1968

Philip Mason, *Prospero's Magic: Some Thoughts on Class and Race*, London, 1962 (Chapter III)

Eldred Jones, *Othello's People*, London, 1965

E. M. W. Tillyard, *The Elizabethan World Picture*, London, 1943, 1952

Chapter 4

Leah Scragg, 'Iago—Vice or Devil', *Shakespeare Survey*, 21, 1968

Felix Raab, *The English Face of Machiavelli*, London, 1964

Wyndham Lewis, *The Lion and the Fox*, 1927, and London, 1966

Lawrence Lerner, 'The Machiavel and the Moor', *Essays in Criticism*, October 1959

Machiavelli, *The Prince*, Penguin edition

Thomas Babington Macaulay, essay on Machiavelli (Everyman), 1961

William Empson, *The Structure of Complex Words*, London, 1951

Kyd's *The Spanish Tragedy*, Marlowe's *The Jew of Malta*, Webster's *The Duchess of Malfi* (referred to in this chapter) are available in *The New Mermaid* series (Ernest Benn), as are Chapman's *Bussy d'Ambois* and other tragedies of villainy and revenge by Ford, Marston, Middleton, Tourneur and others.

Chapter 5

E. E. Stoll, *Art and Artifice in Shakespeare*, London, 1963

F. R. Leavis, 'Diabolical Intellect and the Noble Hero—or The Sentimentalist's Othello', *The Common Pursuit*, London, 1952 and 1962 and Peregrine Paperbacks, 1962

A. C. Bradley, *Shakespearean Tragedy*, 1904, and (paperback) London 1961

Robert Speaight, *Nature in Shakespearian Tragedy*, London, 1955

John Holloway, *The Story of the Night*, London, 1964

H. Granville Barker, Prefaces to Shakespeare's Plays: Vol. IV (paperback, London, 1963) contains *Othello*.

G. Wilson Knight, *The Wheel of Fire*, Oxford, 1930; (paperback) London, 1957

D. A. Traversi, *An Approach to Shakespeare*, London, 1938 (revised, 1957)

H. B. Charlton, *Shakespearian Tragedy*, Cambridge 1948 and (paperback) 1961

David Daiches, 'Guilt and Justice in Shakespeare', *Literary Essays*, Edinburgh, 1955

Select Additional Bibliography (General)

E. A. Abbott, *A Shakespearean Grammar*, London, 1869

C. T. Onions, *A Shakespeare Glossary*, Oxford, 1911, 1953

John Bartlett, *Concordance* to Shakespeare, London, 1894

Mary Cowden-Clark, *Complete Concordance*, Revised Edition, London, 1881

S. T. Coleridge, *Shakespearean Criticism*, Vol. I, London, 1960

A. C. Swinburne, *A Study of Shakespeare*, Oxford, 1880, 1909

Edward Dowden, *Shakespeare, His Mind and Art*, London, 1889

John Bayley, 'Love and Identity', Chapter III (on *Othello*), *The Characters of Love*, London, 1960

Bernard Spivack, *Shakespeare and the Allegory of Evil*, New York, 1958

Jan Kott, *Shakespeare, Our Contemporary*, London, 1967

William Hazlitt, *Characters of Shakespeare's Plays*, London, 1817

Walter Raleigh, Johnson on Shakespeare (selection), London, 1908

J. V. Cunningham, *Woe or Wonder*, Denver, 1951

W. H. Clemen, *The Development of Shakespeare's Imagery* (translated, London, 1951)

R. B. Heilman, 'Modes of Irony in *Othello*', *Shakespeare's Tragedies*, ed. Lawrence Lerner, London, 1963

Henri Fluchère, *Shakespeare, Dramaturge Elizabéthain*, Paris, 1947, 1966 (paperback)

Index